ULYSSES

Ireland Into Film

Series editors:
Keith Hopper (text) and Gráinne Humphreys (images)

Ireland Into Film is the first project in a number of planned collaborations between Cork University Press and the Irish Film Institute. The general aim of this publishing initiative is to increase the critical understanding of 'Irish' Film (i.e. films made in, or about, Ireland). This particular series brings together writers and scholars from the fields of Film and Literary Studies to examine notable adaptations of Irish literary texts.

Other titles available in this series:

The Dead (Kevin Barry)
December Bride (Lance Pettitt)
This Other Eden (Fidelma Farley)
The Informer (Patrick F. Sheeran)
The Quiet Man (Luke Gibbons)
The Field (Cheryl Temple Herr)
Dancing at Lughnasa (Joan FitzPatrick Dean)

Forthcoming titles:

Nora (Gerardine Meaney)
The Butcher Boy (Colin MacCabe)

Ireland Into Film

ULYSSES

Margot Norris

CORK UNIVERSITY PRESS

in association with
THE IRISH FILM INSTITUTE

First published in 2004 by
Cork University Press
Cork
Ireland

British Library Cataloguing in Publication Data
A CIP catalogue record for this book is available from the British Library.

ISBN 1 85918 293 3

Typesetting by Red Barn Publishing, Skeagh, Skibbereen

Printed by ColourBooks Ltd, Baldoyle, Dublin

Ireland Into Film receives financial assistance from
the Arts Council/An Chomhairle Ealaíon and the Irish Film Institute

For my son, Josef Norris, whose love of films and filmmaking when he was young inspired me

CONTENTS

LIST OF ILLUSTRATIONS

Acknowledgements

First, I wish to thank the series editor, Keith Hopper, for giving me this delightful opportunity and for his support and enthusiasm. I first saw the 1967 Joseph Strick film of James Joyce's *Ulysses* while I was an undergraduate student at the University of Florida, and before I had yet read the novel. The film inspired me to read the book, and set me on my way to becoming a life-long scholar of the works of Joyce. I have therefore always had a special interest in the movie and have often wished that I could put my unique double perspective of the film – as novice and as scholar – to some critical use. Keith Hopper gave me just this opportunity. Second, I wish to thank the other series editor, Gráinne Humphreys, for her help with collecting illustrations for my discussion. Since providing the most appropriate images took considerable time, work and technical expertise, I am extremely grateful for this contribution to my text. But I owe her additional thanks for putting me in touch with Joseph Strick, the director of the 1967 film of *Ulysses*. This allowed me to ask hundreds of questions by e-mail, to which I received full, interesting, often funny replies over a period of many months. When Mr Strick visited Los Angeles, he kindly agreed to meet my class at the University of California, at Irvine, and satisfy my students' endless curiosity about his choices in making the film. This was followed by an extensive interview with follow-up phone calls and e-mails, which satisfied my own endless curiosity about how the film was made. In addition, Joseph Strick made his remaining still pictures of the film available to Gráinne Humphreys, even though this entailed the risk of putting them in the post. This generosity on his part, and the openness and candour with which he discussed his project with me, made the writing of this book one of the most pleasurable scholarly experiences of my career as a Joycean. I wish also to thank Jennifer Burns Levin, my industrious and inventive graduate student, for her energy and scholarly talent in helping me track down arcane references. Her formal help and support supplemented and complemented the wonderful informal contribution made by the students of my undergraduate seminar on Joyce's *Ulysses*, taught in winter 2003 at the University of California, Irvine. My students challenged me to ask questions of the text and the film that I had not considered, and made my exploration of the movie a more fruitful collaborative exercise than I could have imagined. In June 2003, I was able to present some of my thoughts about the film at the North American James Joyce Conference in Tulsa, Oklahoma, and the helpful comments and responses of my Joycean colleagues there – especially Thomas Jackson Rice – sharpened my sense of the film even more. And, as always, my fond thanks to my husband, Rowland Davis, for his generous support of all my scholarly efforts.

The editors would also like to thank Antoinette Prout, Ben Cloney, Stephen Moynihan, Sheila Pratschke, Lar Joye, Michael Davitt, Luke Dodd, Dennis Kennedy, Kevin Rockett, Ellen Hazelkorn, Seán Ryder, Paul Sinclair, St Cross College (Oxford), the Irish Film Institute and the Arts Council of Ireland. We owe a special debt of gratitude to Sara Wilbourne, the co-founder of the series, for her unflagging enthusiasm, integrity and commitment.

1

JAMES JOYCE, DRAMA AND CINEMA

James Joyce's background virtually conspired to ensure that his 1922 novel *Ulysses* would eventually be made into a film. When Joyce was a young man and student of literature in Dublin at the turn of the twentieth century, his great love was the genre of drama. But he was also interested in other modes of performance, including popular theatre, pantomimes, opera and musical concerts – all of which eventually played both thematic and formal roles in his fictional works. This interest in the performing arts was eventually extended to the cinema, a young but thriving art form when Joyce first encountered it in Trieste, and which continued to interest him throughout his mature life. The possibility of transforming *Ulysses* into film, therefore, not only occurred to Joyce but was actively explored by him, although its achievement did not take place until 1967, when Joseph Strick produced his black-and-white film version. An exploration of Joyce's early interest in drama, performance and cinema illuminates the historical and cultural currents that contributed to his production of a novel with distinct dramatic and cinematic features. Although cinema is generally treated as a pre-eminently *visual* medium, I hope to infuse my attention to the film of Joyce's *Ulysses* with equal consideration of the role that the *dramatic* – character revelation, enactment of behaviour, dialogue, setting and the like – plays in its adaptation from the novel. Joyce's engagement with drama, both as a genre and as a cultural form, is particularly illuminated by the Irish context in which he received his education. A persistent theme of that education was the sometimes vexed but often productive interplay between modern Irish and Continental culture.

While a student at Belvedere College, a fine Jesuit day-school in Dublin, Joyce participated in amateur theatricals. He parodied the rector of Belvedere in his performance of the hypocritical headmaster, Dr Grimstone, in F. Anstey's play *Vice-Versa*. He later fictionalized this performance in his account of Stephen Dedalus's Belvedere days in *A Portrait of the Artist as a Young Man*. Later, his friend Margaret Sheehy wrote a play called *Cupid's Confidante*, which was performed in 1900 in a café on Grafton Street and a year later at the Antient Concert Rooms. Joyce played the role of the villain, Geoffrey Fortescue, in this second opening, and his performance was lauded in the *Freeman's Journal* (9 January 1901) as 'a revelation of amateur acting'.[1] But drama also became a more serious intellectual preoccupation for Joyce during his education at University College, Dublin. 'Joyce was following the Modern Languages Course, which was seen by most of the students (who were planning professional careers in law and medicine) as "the Ladies Course"', writes Peter Costello.[2] This 'feminine' curriculum was of great benefit to Joyce in giving him access to literary traditions that were both alternative and, in his day, more progressive than the models that English literary history alone offered him. His Eurocentric education exposed him not only to the great nineteenth-century Continental novel tradition, but also to Continental drama, including the experimental and controversial plays of the Norwegian dramatist Henrik Ibsen.

According to Joyce's biographer, Richard Ellmann, Joyce was particularly piqued by a paper delivered to the college's Literary and Historical Society by a student named Arthur Clery, whose subject was 'The Theatre, Its Educational Value'. Clery denounced what he saw as the moral degeneracy of the modern stage, and singled out the work of Henrik Ibsen for special opprobrium. 'The effect of Henrik Ibsen is evil', he is purported to have said in his lecture.[3] This censure can be better understood if we try to imagine how shocking the news of a dramatist whose play openly discussed syphilis on the stage (Ibsen's *Ghosts*) would have appeared to the Victorians. Clery's attack on Ibsen mobilized Joyce's critical talents. He wrote an essay called 'Drama and Life', which he delivered to the Literary and Historical

Society after overcoming the objections of the college president, Father Delany. In this essay Joyce makes a passionate plea for unflinching realism in modern drama: 'Shall we put life – real life – on the stage? No, says the Philistine chorus, for it will not draw. What a blend of thwarted insight and smug commercialism.'[4] The words are strangely prophetic of his own impending struggles as a writer who would face censorship and censure in his attempt to publish his literary vignettes of real Irish life against the folkloric tides of the Irish Revival. 'Life we must accept as we see it before our eyes, men and women as we meet them in the real world, not as we apprehend them in the world of faery', Joyce writes later in the essay.[5] The success of his lecture emboldened the young Joyce to propose to the editor of the *Fortnightly Review* that he would like to write an essay on Ibsen, an offer that led to his first publication of a review of Ibsen's play *When We Dead Awaken*. The essay on 'Ibsen's New Drama' appeared in the journal on 1 April 1900, and earned Joyce his first professional wages of twelve guineas. It also earned him something even more precious: the thanks of Henrik Ibsen himself, conveyed to William Archer, Ibsen's English translator. Joyce was so moved that he wrote Ibsen a brief letter that stated, 'I wish to thank you for kindness in writing to me. I am a young Irishman, eighteen years old, and the words of Ibsen I shall keep in my heart all of my life.'[6]

Richard Ellmann writes, 'Before Ibsen's letter Joyce was an Irishman; after it he was a European.'[7] Joyce began to read Tolstoy, Zola, Flaubert, Huysmans and D'Annunzio and, in 1900 and 1901, bought copies of the plays of Hauptmann, Sudermann and, of course, Ibsen. He had seen Hermann Sudermann's play *Magda* with his parents a year or two earlier. Joyce's early dramatic exposure soon translated into a desire to write drama, and in the summer of 1900 Joyce wrote a play entitled *A Brilliant Career*. This he sent to William Archer, who read it and wrote a painstakingly tactful critique to Joyce in which he praises his talent but calls the play 'wildly impossible' for production on the commercial stage. Joyce destroyed the play a year

3

later – regrettably, since it would be fascinating to see this 'huge fable of politics and pestilence', as Archer called it, teeming with 'such a multitude of figures that Shakespeare himself could scarcely individualize them'.[8] In the summer of 1901, Joyce embarked on a project alternative to writing his own play, by translating two plays of Gerhard Hauptmann's from German into English. The plays were *Vor Sonnenaufgang*, translated as *Before Sunrise*, and *Michael Kramer*, published just a year earlier. Richard Ellmann speculates that Joyce produced the translations in the hope that they would be staged by the Irish Literary Theatre. Joyce was therefore upset to learn in the autumn of 1901 that the theatre was turning chiefly to Irish language plays and plays on Irish mythology. Once again, an imagined cultural affront stirred Joyce's critical juices and he wrote a stinging indictment of the theatre's new policy under the title 'The Day of the Rabblement'. His efforts to publish the piece in the University College magazine once again met the censorship of editor and rector, and Joyce responded by having the piece published at his own expense as a broadside, which also featured Francis Skeffington's essay advocating the admission of women into the university. 'The Day of the Rabblement' makes a powerful argument for the need to make provocative European drama available to Irish audiences and to Irish writers. 'A nation which never advanced as far as a miracle-play affords no literary model to the artist, and he must look abroad', Joyce wrote.[9] Joyce ends the essay by proclaiming Hauptmann as Ibsen's successor and by alluding to a 'third minister' to carry on his tradition, by which he presumably meant himself. The Irish climate of cultural timidity and conservatism that fuelled the protests against William Butler Yeats's *The Countess Cathleen* in 1899, and later, in 1907, against John Millington Synge's *The Playboy of the Western World*, did not fully abate until the onset of the twenty-first century. Only then was Joseph Strick's film of *Ulysses* finally shown in Dublin, thirty-three years after having been banned by Irish censors in 1968, the year after its release.

William Archer's rejection of *A Brilliant Career* may have served as what we now call a 'reality check' on Joyce's youthful dramatic ambitions. Theatre – like film – is notoriously expensive and risky to mount, and fiction may have come to seem to him a more manageable genre that could none the less incorporate dramatic elements. Several of Joyce's *Dubliners* stories have a distinctly theatrical or cinematic cast to them. 'Ivy Day in the Committee Room' in particular has the character of a one-act play, as a number of critics have pointed out, with the narration serving chiefly to give stage directions for entrances and exits while the bulk of the story consists of dialogue and conversation. The story 'Two Gallants' describes figures with virtually cinematic attention to their visual exhibition, as when it introduces Lenehan, who, we learn, 'wore an amused listening face'. The text tells us not what Lenehan hears but how 'the narrative to which he listened made constant waves of expression break forth over his face from the corners of his nose and eyes and mouth. Little jets of wheezing laughter followed one another out of his convulsed body. His eyes, twinkling with cunning enjoyment, glanced at every moment toward his companion's face.'[10] A film actor could scarcely hope for more explicit directions for enactment than this. Alan Spiegel finds even earlier evidence of cinematographic writing in one of the lost sketches by the adolescent Joyce entitled 'Silhouettes', which his brother Stanislaus Joyce remembers in his memoir. The sketch was apparently a first-person description of a viewer looking up at a back-lit window that functions effectively as a movie screen. The viewer sees 'two figures in violent agitation on a lowered window-blind illuminated from within, the burly figure of a man, staggering and threatening with upraised fist, and the smaller sharp-faced figure of a nagging woman. A blow is struck and the light goes out.'[11] Spiegel notes that, since the sketch must have been written between 1893 and 1898, '[I]t is almost certain that young Joyce could have had no knowledge of the cinema since at the time there was almost certainly no cinema in Dublin. And yet in its optical invention and treatment of time and space, the passage is presented in a mode that could only be described as cinematographic.'[12]

Although we do not know where or when Joyce saw his first film, we do know that there were two movie houses in Trieste during the time the Joyces lived there. There could have been an occasional special film exhibition in Dublin while Joyce resided there. But Ellmann credits Joyce's young sister Eva with giving him an idea for a business scheme, when – delighted with the films she saw in Trieste – she noted how odd it was that Dublin had no cinema.[13] Joyce saw a commercial opportunity and put himself into contact with a small group of Triestine businessmen to see if they would back the venture of establishing a cinema in Dublin. In the fall of 1909 Joyce travelled to Dublin to organize a 'cinematograph exhibition' of Continental one-reel films, accompanied by a small orchestra or piano, in preparation for the opening of a theatre there to be called *Cinematograph Volta*. The first programme included Pathé's *The Bewitched Castle* and *The First Paris Orphanage*, Mario Caserini's *Beatrice Cenci*, which Peter Costello calls a landmark of Italian cinema at that time, and a comedy called *The Devilled Crab*.[14] The venture had a promising start under Joyce's management and earned excellent newspaper reviews, but it declined when he returned to Trieste and his place was taken by one of the Italian investors, Francesco Novak, who spoke no English. Within a short time the Volta was sold at a loss. By the time Joyce became peripherally involved in another, less savory cinema scheme, World War I had broken out, Joyce and his family had moved to Zurich and Joyce had completed his own play, a drama called *Exiles*. Begun with notes in 1913 and finally published in 1918, the writing and completion of Joyce's only play coincided with the drafting of his great novel, *Ulysses*. The second cinema enterprise was the brainchild of a would-be filmmaker named Jules Martin, who tried to engage Joyce in working on a screenplay called *Wine, Woman, and Song*.[15] Martin's plan was to entice wealthy women to enroll in a *Kino Schule* whose instruction would ostensibly train them for cinematic acting careers. Suitably trained, they would then be offered a chance to star in one of Martin's films for a fee. This abortive collaboration with Martin may have been the source of the rumour Joyce reported to Harriet Shaw Weaver in 1921 when he told her 'A man from Liverpool told me he had heard that I was the owner of several cinema theatres all over Switzerland.'[16] In actuality, Joyce extricated himself from Martin's scam and turned his interest instead to the busy theatrical scene that enlivened Zurich during World War I. He not only took in a great deal of modern drama, including productions by Max Reinhardt and the plays of Büchner, Strindberg, Franz Wedekind and René Schickele, but he also worked to get *Exiles* staged.

These efforts too ended up embroiling Joyce in a first-class fiasco. An actor friend named Claude Sykes encouraged Joyce to help him form an acting troupe that would produce English plays in Switzerland – a proposal Joyce seized enthusiastically as a way of possibly securing a staging of *Exiles*. The company was called the English Players and for its first production – significantly by an Irish playwright – they mounted Oscar Wilde's *The Importance of Being Earnest*. Joyce had unfortunately engaged a young man working at the British consulate named Henry Carr to play one of the starring roles. Since Carr was technically an amateur, he was paid very little – an outcome that vexed the young man, since he had incurred expenses for his costume of trousers, a new hat and a pair of gloves. When Carr claimed reimbursement for these expenses, Joyce angrily demanded a refund for tickets Carr had been given to sell. The dispute ended in a public shouting match that escalated to a point where Joyce proceeded to sue Carr, first for ticket repayment, and then for libel. The business went through two trials before Joyce finally withdrew his complaint, only to face distraint for refusing to pay court costs and damages.[17] This incident later became the focal point of Tom Stoppard's *Travesties* (1989), a play set in 1917 Zurich when Tristan Tzara, Lenin and Joyce all lived in the city. Joyce was probably not cut out to be either a businessman or a producer, nor, in the eyes of many critics, a playwright – although *Exiles* was finally produced in Munich in 1919. Yet he clearly brought dramatic and cinematographic experiences and talents to his fiction, and these flowered in *Ulysses*.

By the time *Ulysses* was finally published in 1922, the Joyces were living in Paris and enjoying the work's status as a *cause célèbre*. During this time Joyce was clearly seeing a great deal of film, and beginning to use the cinema as a trope for what he saw in his mind's eye when cataracts and eye operations diminished his sight. In 1924 he explained to Harriet Shaw Weaver that 'whenever I am obliged to lie with my eyes closed I see a cinematograph going on and on and it brings back to my memory things I had almost forgotten'. Later in the year, he wrote to Weaver again after his cataract surgery, 'I am still bandaged up – had prolonged cinema nights and am *extrêmement fatigué*.'[18] The possibility of turning *Ulysses* into a film seems to have occurred to Joyce relatively early. Within two years of the book's publication, Joyce had to consider the various problems and possibilities that attended the prospect of translating the novel into other languages, foremost French. Ellmann reports, 'At first he had thought, as he told Daniel Hummel, that the book could not be translated into another language, but might be translated into another medium, that of film.'[19] A few years later Joyce was to have a meeting with one of the greatest filmmakers of the twentieth century, the legendary Russian director Sergei Eisenstein. The fullest information on this meeting is presented from the perspective of Eisenstein in Gösta Werner's 1990 essay in the *James Joyce Quarterly*. Much of her information is drawn from Eisenstein's writings and memoirs, researched at the Eisenstein Museum and Archives in Moscow.

According to Werner, Eisenstein made a trip to Berlin in August of 1929 with two of his collaborators, Gregory Alexandrov and the cameraman Eduard Tisse, which turned into an extended sojourn abroad and included lectures in London, Brussels, Rotterdam and

Paris. Eisenstein had read Joyce's *A Portrait of the Artist as a Young Man* and *Ulysses* earlier, and had already begun to refer to Joyce in his lectures and notes and to praise '*Ulysses* as a particularly suitable basic [*sic*] for training visual consciousness'.[20] The meeting between Joyce and Eisenstein on 30 November 1929 seems to have occurred at Eisenstein's initiative. It was arranged by a young Russian film technician named Boris Lyakhovskiy, with the assistance of Sylvia Beach. Werner found pasted into the 1928 signed copy of *Ulysses* that Joyce gave Eisenstein at the end of the meeting the telephone message from Lyakhovskiy. It alerted him that 'Mlle Beach will make every effort to arrange the meeting but wants Monsieur Eisenstein to telephone today between 4 and 7 P.M. to Monsieur James Joyce, Segur 45–20, in order to fix a time for tomorrow's meeting'.[21] Later, in his memoirs, Eisenstein would pay a particularly affectionate tribute to Sylvia Beach and her bookstore, *Shakespeare and Company:*

> Here, it is Joyceana.
> Joyce's works.
> I greatly loved this quiet street.
> I greatly loved this modest quiet bookshop
> and the grey-haired Sylvia Beach.
> I often dropped in on her.
> Sat in her back room.

And gazed at the walls for ages; they were hung with innumerable faded photographs.
An idiosyncratic pantheon of literature.[22]

The meeting between Joyce and Eisenstein occurred, but there is no indication that the men discussed a possible filming of *Ulysses*. Eisenstein's memoirs tell us that at this meeting Joyce read to him from *Ulysses*, and they listened to a gramophone recording of Joyce reading from 'Anna Livia Plurabelle', which Eisenstein could follow on a copy of the text pages that had been enlarged to compensate for

Joyce's poor eyesight. They must have spoken of Eisenstein's films. 'He just asked me – entreated me – to show him my films; he seems interested in the experiments with film language that I am carrying out (just as I am interested in his literary experiments of a similar nature).'[23] In an earlier essay Eisenstein identified the films Joyce asked to see as *Potemkin* (1925) and *October* (1927). Eisenstein's memoirs also explain the darkened room that in Hans Richter's report to Ellmann had made Eisenstein think of the meeting as a 'ghost experience'.[24] Clearly no lights were provided because Joyce's near-blindness made them irrelevant. The ultimate irony of this meeting was that one of the greatest artists in the visual medium of film was encountering one of the greatest writers of prose, who had virtually no sight. Eisenstein describes how Joyce on parting waved his hands and groped strangely along the walls when trying to help Eisenstein find his coat. 'Then it suddenly strikes me how blind this man is, and I think that this "outer" blindness is a condition for – an explanation of – his "inner" perspicacity, as when describing "inner life" in *Ulysses* and *A Portrait of the Artist as a Young Man*. I am ashamed of myself.'[25] Before parting, Joyce wrote a dedication to Eisenstein in a copy of *Ulysses*. When Eisenstein returned to the hotel, he found that Joyce's inscribed 'dedication as well as the date, 30 November 1929, is practically illegible'.

The meeting made an enormous impression on Eisenstein, who continued to think of Joyce as 'a veritable colossus', and whose memoirs state simply, 'I had a long-standing love of *Ulysses*'.[26] But the meeting seems also to have made an impression on Joyce. Apparently it was after this that Joyce told Eugene Jolas that 'for a possible future filming of *Ulysses* he could only think of two persons who were qualified as directors: Eisenstein and Walter Ruttmann'.[27] Ruttmann's qualification included not only his status as an avant-garde documentarian, but, more specifically, his production of *Berlin: The Symphony of a City* (1927), which captured the urban life of the vibrant German city in a stream of associated pictures from the morning to

the nightfall of a single day. However, neither Eisenstein nor
Ruttmann were ever seriously engaged to explore a possible filming
of *Ulysses*. Eisenstein went on to Hollywood not long after his
meeting with Joyce in the hope of making a film of Theodore
Dreiser's *American Tragedy* for Paramount. Why did Eisenstein never
consider making a film of *Ulysses* when he had such unbounded
admiration for the novel? Perhaps chiefly because he returned to the
Soviet Union in 1933. Emily Tall reminds us of the violent outburst
against James Joyce at the August 1934 First International Congress
of Soviet Writers in Moscow, and of the climate of censure this
created for Joyce's work.[28] The attack was led by Karl Radek, a Soviet
Party spokesman who was liquidated three years later by Stalin,
according to Jeffrey Segall.[29] Curiously, Radek's most virulent rhetoric
resorts precisely to cinematographic imagery in condemning Joyce's
literary technique. Calling Joyce's work 'a heap of dung', Radek
depicted it as 'teeming with worms and photographed by a motion-
picture camera through a microscope'. A few months later in
November, Sergei Eisenstein presented a lecture on James Joyce to
the State Institute of Cinematography in which he deplored the
effects of Radek's attack. 'What did his speech lead to? His speech
discredited Joyce terribly and as a result Joyce probably won't be
translated', he lamented.[30] Eisenstein was right, in the main. Tall
reports that, although ten chapters of *Ulysses* were translated during
the period of the Popular Front in 1935–36, translation was halted
and not discussed again in Russia for the next forty years. Eisenstein's
filmmaking was relegated chiefly to epic glorifications of Russian
heroes during the Stalin years (*Alexander Nevksy* and *Ivan the Terrible*)
and he died in 1948.

It was therefore an American studio, Warner Brothers, which
contacted Joyce's agent, Ralph Pinker, in 1932 to seek the film rights
to *Ulysses*. Before Joyce could give a definitive answer, he heard that
press notices in the United States were already discussing the
impending filming. He consequently had his friend Paul Léon

transmit a firm refusal on the Warner Brothers project to Pinker. Léon wrote, 'I have taken the matter up with Mr Joyce who in fact tells me that he is in principle opposed to the filming of *Ulysses* and would like the news in the paper to be denied'. Leon goes on to point out that, even though the Random House publisher Bennett Cerf felt that a film version would enhance sales of the book, Joyce was not swayed. '[Cerf] naturally takes the material point of view, Mr Joyce on the contrary takes the literary point of view and is therefore opposed to the filming as irrealisable.'[31] The apparent contradiction between this refusal and Joyce's more exploratory and speculative stance at other times is best addressed by Thomas Burkdall, who invokes the context of this specific letter: 'Given the legal tone of the missive and the fact that it seems clearly designed to prevent premature "press news . . . about the forthcoming film of *Ulysses*" (and ultimately to thwart piracy of the film rights), it seems imprudent to take these as Joyce's artistic opinions about adapting the novel to the screen'.[32]

But even though the Warner Brothers plan fell through, explorations of possible cinematic projects continued without leading to realization. Stuart Gilbert was encouraged to try producing a screenplay of the novel. In 1934, Joyce's son George also began to promote the filming of *Ulysses* and particularly urged Joyce to consider scenarios produced by the poets Louis Zukofsky and S. J. Reisman.[33] Joyce received and read the proposed screenplays and, in an October 1935 letter to George, commented on their choice of Charles Laughton to play Leopold Bloom. 'He seems too "Aryan" to me', Joyce noted. His own inclination was to consider the English actor George Arliss, who had portrayed Disraeli in the 1929 film: 'I am going to see Arliss who was, they say, a good Disraeli'.[34] According to Joyce's friends Eugene and Maria Jolas, Joyce also admired the work of the documentary filmmaker Robert Flaherty. Flaherty's films included the famous 1922 silent film about Eskimos, *Nanook of the North*, as well as the 1934 *Man of Aran*. Joyce apparently discussed

Man of Aran at length with the Jolases, and Flaherty became another filmmaker Joyce considered as a contender for filming *Ulysses*.[35] But nothing came of any of these possibilities. Joyce continued to see films throughout the 1930s, in spite of his poor eyesight. Lucie Noël, the wife of Paul Léon, tells a funny story of attending Hedy Lamarr's erotic and controversial 1933 film *Ecstasy* (dir. Gustav Machatý) with Joyce, in order to serve as his 'seeing eye': 'The movie was *Exstase*, in which Hedy Lamarr ran around the countryside perfectly beautiful and quite nude . . . The picture was quite erotic and I was quite embarrassed because I had to explain much of the action to Joyce.' One can imagine that Joyce, the author of Gerty MacDowell's and Molly Bloom's erotic fantasies, would have been vastly amused by this need for female translation of erotica. Mary Colum also witnessed an electric meeting between Joyce and Marlene Dietrich, who was accompanied by her friend Erich Maria Remarque. Joyce told her he had seen her in *The Blue Angel* and Dietrich is said to have replied, 'Then, monsieur, you saw the best of me.'[36]

Ulysses would not be filmed until many years after Joyce's death, when his early interest in drama and his grasp of cinematic representation would infuse and inform the possibilities of its adaptation, while the shifting styles, the narrative experiments and rhetorical play would defy and limit translation into the visual medium. Joyce's Continental engagement with the cinema during so much of his working life would translate into a trail of thematic, verbal and formal allusions in his most avant-garde masterpiece, his 1939 *Finnegans Wake*. As early as his 1969 *Reader's Guide to 'Finnegans Wake'*, William York Tindall alerted readers to Joyce's numerous allusions to cinematography as well as to specific films in his last work. These included *My Man Godfrey* (dir. Gregory La Cava, 1936), *Birth of a Nation* (dir. D. W. Griffith, 1915) and *Mr Deeds Goes to Town* (dir. Frank Capra, 1936). Joyce also extensively glossed an old Hollywood scandal known as 'Daddy Browning and the Peaches' in *Finnegans Wake*.[37] Indeed, Peter Costello claims that '*Finnegans Wake*, in which the new medium is mentioned in fiction for the first time, is completely televisual'.[38] But if *Finnegans Wake* can be thought to have predicted television, a medium Joyce would not have seen in his lifetime, many of the formal features of *Ulysses* might be thought to have predicted the cinema, which was in its infancy at the time of the novel's setting but which was undergoing rapid maturation at the time of the novel's writing.

2

JOSEPH STRICK AND THE MODERN AVANT-GARDE

More than twenty-five years after James Joyce's death *Ulysses* was at last made into a film. The filmmaker, an independent not affiliated with a studio, was Joseph Strick, whose career up to the making of *Ulysses* had fortuitously prepared him for just this project. Joseph Strick was born in Braddock, Pennsylvania, near Pittsburgh, in 1923 and grew up in Pennsylvania. His father was a Jewish immigrant from Poland who worked for the steel industry and had a talent for engineering and inventing. The family had great respect for the arts, and Strick's father smuggled a copy of *Ulysses* into the United States from France while it was still banned. The US ban was not lifted until

Plate 1. Joseph Strick

1933 – eleven years after *Ulysses* was published – when the Hon. Judge John M. Woolsey ruled in the New York District Court that the novel was not obscene. Joseph Strick told interviewer Stephen Watts that his parents enjoyed keeping the book on view at home in the hope of stirring up debate with visitors. They challenged friends and argued with them if they judged the novel 'dirty'. Strick's father showed himself to be a wise reader of *Ulysses*. 'It's about life and people – you and me and all the rest', he used to say.[1] To young Joseph himself the book was initially just 'like an artifact, an interesting object that lay around the house', but when he was sixteen, he picked it up and finally read *Ulysses* himself. Watts reports: 'He didn't understand it but was fascinated. He had found something completely new, and he says he has been finding new things in it ever since.'

Joseph Strick read a lot of plays when he was in his teens, but he also read much fiction by Sinclair Lewis and Joseph Conrad. He would try to find and read works reviewed favourably in the *New York Times*: 'To see films not available in Philadelphia I would take the train to New York and see those playing in the Museum of Modern Art which was really my film school.'[2] He entered UCLA in 1941 and studied science, because he was convinced 'that physics would win the war'. While at UCLA, Strick met Barney Rosset, who would ten years later found Grove Press – for which Strick would eventually serve as an outside director. Military service in the United States Air Force fragmented Strick's education: a summer session at Penn, night classes at Denver University, courses at the Woman's College of North Carolina in Greensboro, Gettysburg College, a correspondence course at the University of Indiana. But his interest in filmmaking began through his work as an aerial photographer with the Air Force during World War II. During the long hours of anti-submarine duty, he had time to experiment with the still and moving picture photographic equipment and he occasionally made short joke movies to entertain his friends. After leaving the Air Force in 1946, he went to Los Angeles, where he began work as a copy boy on the *Los Angeles Times* and tried to figure out his way to directing films. He bought an army surplus 35mm camera and began photographing muscle men and acrobats on the beach of Venice, California, and working with Irving Lerner to turn the scenes into a short documentary. The product was *Muscle Beach*, which was shown at the Cannes Film Festival in 1949 – although, according to Strick, none of the judges attended its showing. *Muscle Beach* was followed by some years of work in television, as well as another film, *The Big Break*, which was released in 1953. During these years, however, Joseph Strick began working on an ambitious new film. This was the highly experimental docudrama, *The Savage Eye*, which was released in Britain in 1959 and in the US in 1960. The film starred Barbara Baxley, Herschel Bernardi and Gary Merill and, in a loose narrative, told the story of a divorcee who comes to Los Angeles to find a new life. The film used techniques of *cinéma vérité* that gave the camera status as a 'character' in the film and foregrounded its role in producing perspective and point of view. *The Savage Eye* won awards from the Venice Film Festival and the British Academy, and is still considered groundbreaking by many critics.

Four years later, in 1963, Strick, together with Ben Maddow, made a film of Jean Genet's 1956 drama, *The Balcony*. The play had caused a stir, and Strick saw it during its first run, liked it and decided to pursue the film rights. He tells how he made contact with Jean Genet: 'I was a director of Grove Press through my friendship with Barney Rosset which began at UCLA in 1941, and knew their books and some of their authors. I approached Genet through his London agent, Rosica Colins, and worked with Genet on the treatment of *The Balcony* for two months in 1963.'³ The film starred Shelley Winters, Peter Falk, Lee Grant, Ruby Dee and Leonard Nimoy – a stunning cast, although only Shelley Winters was well known at the time. Peter Falk was just beginning to be known, as was Leonard Nimoy, whose *Star Trek* roles commenced a few years later. Ruby Dee was just coming to prominence with her role in the 1961 *A Raisin in the Sun*. The actress Lee Grant had been on the brink of a highly promising film career in the early 1950s when she was blacklisted by the House Un-American Committee after refusing to testify against her husband, Arnold Manoff. The film was shot in six weeks – much too fast, according to Strick. The budget was $150,000, with all of the actors and technicians on the film working at minimum union wages. *The Balcony*, set in a brothel in which three men enact erotic scenes with prostitutes that project their social ambitions for the roles of bishop, general and judge, was filmed in a hallucinatory style that foreshadows the Nighttown episode in Strick's film of *Ulysses*. Strick's choice of a play that was initially staged in a private London club because it was considered too pornographic for the theatrical stage also foreshadows his willingness to tackle controversial avant-garde materials likely to rile censors. Jean Genet himself loved the film, Joseph Strick told Michael Dwyer in 2000.[4] He was particularly taken by the notion of the film studio as a brothel. Genet also liked Strick's idea of using documentary footage to suggest the revolution raging outside the brothel. In spite of its provocative story, *The Balcony* was honoured with an Academy Award nomination for Best Black-and-White Cinematography in 1964.

Even before making *The Balcony*, Joseph Strick tried to get the film rights for *Ulysses*. Although Warner Brothers had been refused the film rights to *Ulysses* at Joyce's direction in 1932, the Joyce Estate was considering bids for them in 1961. However, the producer Jerry Wald, supported by Twentieth Century Fox, opened the bidding with $75,000 – far beyond Strick's means – and thereby secured the rights to the film. During the previous year Wald had successfully adapted D. H. Lawrence's novel *Sons and Lovers* for the screen, and he may therefore have felt ready to take on the adaptation of an even more challenging and controversial modern novel. Although Wald planned to have Jack Cardiff, his director for *Sons and Lovers*, direct the film, Joseph Strick tried to convince Wald to let him direct it. But Wald, Strick reports, was too preoccupied with his work on *Return to Peyton Place* to make a decision. A year later Jerry Wald died, and Joseph

Strick thereafter learned, while in transit from London to New York by plane, that the film rights had reverted to the Joyce estate. According to Stephen Watts, 'The moment he got off the plane, he phoned London.' The negotiations with the Joyce estate for the rights were protracted, but Strick – in the throes of a divorce after nineteen years of marriage and three children – remembers that he was treated with great courtesy and consideration. Working with Anne Munro-Kerr of the Society of Authors (who managed the James Joyce Estate until Joyce's grandson Stephen Joyce assumed leadership), an arrangement was made to let Strick secure the rights with a $10,000 down payment followed by a payment schedule.[5] Unlike Jerry Wald, who had been assigned a Joyce consultant, Joseph Strick was entrusted with the film rights with no such stipulation. Strick had met and spoken to Harry Levin, but he chiefly relied on wide general reading of *Ulysses* criticism rather than on scholarly consultation for his interpretations. He found Edmund Wilson particularly helpful.[6]

Raising money to make the film turned out to be frustratingly difficult, even though Strick's earlier films had made money. In his 11 November 2000 interview with the *Irish Times*, Strick explained his principle of independent filmmaking to Michael Dwyer: 'My pattern always has been to buy the material and develop it and then go to the studios. If you don't do that, you are victimized by the studio's investment and their control, and to me it's ludicrous to make a movie if I don't have control, if I don't have final cut, which very few film-makers get. I've just seen too many awful situations.' For the financing of *Ulysses* Strick hoped for a reliable backer and therefore first approached the major companies who could be relied on to pay the bills. He says, 'I remember vividly that after *The Balcony* opened so well I solicited Columbia Pictures and when their chief, Leo Jaffe, asked why they should finance an art film based on a book they couldn't read, I replied that *The Savage Eye* and *The Balcony* had produced very unusually high results for very low investments. He countered with, "Anyone can catch lightning in a bottle!"[7] After the major studios turned him down, Strick turned to the independents. His luck with *Ulysses* changed when he accidentally ran into theatre owner, producer and distributor Walter Reade, Jr, whom he had met while working on *The Balcony*. Reade had been interested in the *Ulysses* project when it had been with Jerry Wald and was delighted to learn that Strick now held the rights. Joseph Strick describes Reade as 'a big, bluff man who wore a fresh carnation every day', whose father had collected a chain of movie theatres and 'palaces' on the New Jersey shore and in Manhattan. Reade's entrepreneurial genius led him to begin importing foreign films, which had few outlets in the US at the time – an effort that brought him into association with British Lion Films. This consortium of five British producers had acquired Shepperton Studios, 'the best of the suburban London film factories', according to Strick. Walter Reade became the sixth member of the consortium, whose arrangement was that each of the six directors had the right to name two films of their choice for production.[8] Reade named *Ulysses*, to the disgust of the Boulting brothers, who held one of the directorial positions and hated the idea. The Boultings, who had had a great success in 1959 with their comedy *I'm All Right, Jack*, thought the script for *Ulysses* was too explicit. When told that the script came virtually word for word from Joyce's novel, they were unimpressed and declined to read the book. '"You'll make it," said Roy Boulting, "over my dead body"', Strick remembers.[9] In the end the contract stipulated that the film would have to receive a certificate of approval from the British censor before release. Since approval could be granted only to the filmed version, not the script, Strick proceeded with the filming, even though he anticipated difficulty with getting money from British Lion during the shooting.

Ideally, Strick would have made a film as long as the action of *Ulysses* itself – about eighteen and three-quarter hours. Barring that, he would have made *Ulysses* as a trilogy, 'but of course I couldn't raise a lead cent for that'.[10] He told Michael Dwyer in 2000, 'I couldn't raise the money for the 18 hours, so I worked within the money I could raise'. In the end, Joseph Strick says, the 'budget for *Ulysses* was $450,000 and we shot for three months'.[11] But while the budgetary constraints dictated the film's conventional length of 132 minutes, the decision to set the film in 1960s Dublin rather than at the turn of the century was both a pragmatic and an artistic choice. 'That one day in 1904 which Joyce so voluminously describes could not be recreated in modern Dublin even on an epic budget, so there was no question of making a period picture,' Strick told Stephen Watts in 1966. He insists that the decision to update the time of the novel in the film was not specifically financial: 'I don't like to hide behind budget constraints. I knew what the stakes were in attempting *Ulysses* and if I've failed in some way I would not dodge responsibility. I could have raised more money if I'd worked at it another five years, I think. I was interested in the idea that if Joyce had taken a liberty with over 2,000 years, I could take the same liberty with 60.'[12] His choice of little-known actors also reflected an artistic choice rather than a financial constraint. Strick had seen Milo O'Shea in a Dublin revue in 1964 and instantly said: 'There's Bloom.' He had seen Barbara Jefford play Shakespeare with the Old Vic in Los Angeles some years before and arranged for her to play Madame Irma in *The Balcony*. Difficulties with her agents aborted that plan, but Strick, who considers her a great actress, was delighted to cast her as Molly Bloom in *Ulysses*. Interestingly, Barbara Jefford's only film experience prior to *Ulysses* was to lend her voice to a Czech animation film of *A Midsummer Night's Dream*, and to the voice of Tatiana, played by the Italian actress Daniela Bianchi, in the 1963 film *From Russia With Love*. Her haunting voice, speaking Molly's thoughts from the 'Penelope' chapter of the novel, was recorded before the film was shot, because it would inspire the aesthetic texture of the rest, according to Strick. Michael Dwyer calls the cast of *Ulysses* a veritable 'who's who of Irish acting', since virtually all the performers were

Irish, with the exception of Jefford and Graham Lines (Haines), who were British, and Maurice Roëves, who played Stephen Dedalus. Roëves, who grew up in Newcastle-upon-Tyne in northeastern England and was educated in Glasgow, calls himself both a Geordie and a Scots Glaswegian.[13] In addition to having Milo O'Shea play Leopold Bloom, Strick cast T. P. McKenna as Buck Mulligan, Anna Manahan as Bella Cohen, Maureen Potter as Josie Breen, Martin Dempsey as Simon Dedalus and Joe Lynch as Blazes Boylan. According to the Stephen Watts interview, the top salary for the actors was '£100 a week, plus percentages if and when'.[14]

Joseph Strick served as director for the film and co-wrote the script with Fred Haines, a collaboration that would eventually earn them an Academy Award nomination for Best Adapted Screenplay in 1967. 'On the problems of scripting, he holds that it was not a writing but an editing job', Stephen Watts reports, because the script is '99 per cent unadulterated Joyce'.[15] Strick told Michael Dwyer in 2000: 'I made it just from the text . . . There are no new words. Who's going to rewrite Joyce? I know nobody that good.' Strick maintains that the only language he and Fred Haines added to the script were occasional 'connectives' needed to smooth transitions between scenes. Their chief work as writers of the screenplay was the work of selection: deciding which parts of narration, monologue and dialogue to include in the film and which to exclude. 'It hurt to cut so much', Strick told Watts. But what was retained was substantially pure Joyce. This fidelity to making a film of *Ulysses* in the actual language of the novel's text is remarkable when compared to the liberties often taken in adapting novels to film. For instance, John Huston's cinematic adaptation of Joyce's short story 'The Dead' diverged in significant ways from the original without the necessity to compress that faced Strick.[16] Strick's rigour in giving Joyce's language the principal auditory voice in his film may somewhat differentiate his *Ulysses* from the new cinematic version of the novel, *Bl,.m* (dir. Sean Walsh, 2003). According to Paul Cullen's article in the *Irish Times* (19 June 2001), the new film's director intends his version of *Ulysses* to function as 'mainstream cinema' and has cut large sections of Joyce's text. He has also rearranged events, putting Molly Bloom's famous soliloquy at the start, rather than the end, of the action.'[17] Ironically, Strick's adherence to Joyce's language and scenes provoked criticism of its 'literalism' by some reviewers, causing Pauline Kael to complain that 'The movie is an act of homage in the form of readings from the book plus illustrated slides.'[18] But the Academy Award nomination for adaptation speaks to the script's impressive quality. 'I was sitting there at the ceremony,' Strick told Michael Dwyer, 'composing my speech, as we all do, and planning to give all the credit to Joyce. I was sitting next to Warren Beatty, who was just as tense. He was there with *Bonnie and Clyde*. We were so high on adrenalin.' In the end, that year's big Oscar winner, *In the Heat of the Night*, also took the award for best adapted screenplay in 1967.

A number of highly talented people worked on the film with Joseph Strick. His editor, Reginald Mills, had edited *Black Narcissus* in 1947 and received an Academy Award nomination for his editing of the 1948 film, *The Red Shoes*. He went on to edit the 1968 Franco Zeffirelli film of *Romeo and Juliet*. The unusual original music in *Ulysses* was composed by Stanley Myers, who also researched Matthew Hodgart and Mabel Worthington's *Songs in the Work of James Joyce*[19] and other period music that plays a role in the novel. Stanley Myers' most famous composition in later years was the theme to Michael Cimino's 1978 film, *The Deer Hunter*. The cinematographer for *Ulysses* was a Viennese named Wolfgang Suschitzky, who worked chiefly in Great Britain. Bosley Crowther comments on the 'beautifully utilized camera' in the film, which suffused its scenes 'with the grayness and mellowness of Dublin'.[20] The choice to make the film in black and white was again based on aesthetic considerations rather than budgetary ones, according to Strick. He liked black and white and had made all of his previous films in that format. 'I've never liked the color emulsions available to us, except for the Agfa, more pastel film stocks. Black and white film has all those gradations, all those nuances . . . I could have raised the extra bit of money to make the film in color: it would have been about 5%, but I didn't want to face the extra compromising that color entails', he wrote.[21] *Ulysses* had close to 2,000 camera set-ups, compared to the average film, which has three or four hundred, Strick told Stephen Watts in 1966. The normal sequence of shots in ordinary filming was inadequate for the strategies required to approximate Joyce's stream of consciousness in the film. Strick explains:

> It would be lovely to try a long, single-take, truly associative, many-story-elemented shot but I chose to try it in simple cuts, simply shot, with an attempt to get each shot to have the clarity, the focus, the composition, the . . . oh, well you know . . . the gestalt of the particular moment Joyce gave us in the text.

Strick had begun the filming before all the financial wrangles with British Lion were fully resolved. As a result, money was held up during the filming and Strick faced the possibility of having to borrow against his house should it become necessary. But he trusted British Lion's Managing Director, David Kinsgley, and its Chairman, Arnold Goodman, to ensure that the agreements to date would be honoured. In the end he remembers being saved by a three-week Irish bank strike, during which cheques could not be negotiated. 'We were able to issue cheques in merry fashion for I was sure that the Boultings would be scared by the possibility of a scandal should they not agree to Goodman's ruling that the film must go forward.'[22] British Lion did honour the cheques after the strike ended and Strick was able to complete filming. Once the film was edited, the problem of getting a censor's certificate became urgent. The film's faithfulness to the text made Strick confident that he would not have censorship problems in the United States. The 1933 decision by Judge Woolsey pronouncing that the text of *Ulysses* was not obscene made it difficult to imagine that the same language on film could be judged otherwise. 'Can the position be that what is all right in a book is not all right in a film?' Strick asked.[23] The British Board of Film Censors was another matter. In Britain, film censorship began when a blaze in a fire-trap cinema killed a number of people and thereafter local agencies, often fire brigades, were made responsible for licensing movie houses. While local authorities licensed film venues, the British Board of Film Censors ruled on moral and legal matters with respect to films.

Joseph Strick had an early encounter with this body when British Lion, which was the United Kingdom distributor for *The Balcony*, submitted that film for approval in 1963. At that time Strick met one of the censors, a Mr John Trevelyan, 'scion of the family of historians and later to be knighted', according to the director. As Strick recalls him, Trevelyan was 'a pleasant man when not ruffled, given to letting his cigarette ash grow too long and to assuming that his scale of values was reasonable and irrefutable'.[24] Strick remembers that *The Balcony* made Trevelyan very nervous, and he stipulated that it should be sent to local authorities and councils to be vetted prior to formal approval by the Board. The London County Council approved it without fuss, as did a number of other local groups, including one village fire brigade, and *The Balcony* was given an X certificate. However, getting censors' approval for *Ulysses* was complicated by John Trevelyan's friendship with a number of the British Lion executives who disliked the film and hoped to block the certificate. When he saw the filmed *Ulysses*, Trevelyan demanded twenty-nine cuts. While trying to figure out how to respond, a young American assistant to a BBC TV news feature program called '24 Hours' offered to run the cut excerpts on the programme and found that viewers were not offended. Nevertheless, Lady Dartmouth (who later became Lady Spencer, the stepmother of Princess Diana) publicly denounced the film to the London City Council, according to Strick. Without either having read the book or seen extracts of the film, she warned that if the film were released there would be 'public lovemaking in Piccadilly Circus', according to Strick. 'I replied that the film was pretty good, but not that good.'[25] All of this media attention had generated a great deal of publicity for the not-yet-approved or released film. Strick now chose strategically to release the censor's version of the film, but used his right to make the final cut to blank out the scenes at places where a cut was ordered. He filled these blanked spaces with 'terrible noises' on the sound track in order to make the cut version of the film impossible to release. Strick relates how he sent this defaced version to John Trevelyan for approval and received an immediate phone call asking, ' "What have you done to your beautiful film?" British Lion capitulated and the film was released uncut.' The film ran for a year in London at the Academy Theatre on Oxford Street, and that run alone recuperated the entire cost of the film's production.

Strick narrates Walter Reade's clever distribution gambit in the United States:

> When the film was finished Walter set about to capitalize on every promotional aspect. He had a film without stars, without an exploitable story line and he decided he would make use of the inevitable censoring attacks. He organized 150 theaters to show the film for a three day, reserved performance run on the notion that the film could be seen before censors had a chance to act. The prevailing price of a movie ticket was $3 at the time and Walter decided on a $5.50 price. The present-day equivalent would be about $27.50. When the exhibitors saw the film a week before its release, two thirds of the engagements were cancelled by nervous managements. Then the film opened, got extraordinary notices, sold out and we eventually played in at least 1,000 cinemas in the US alone.[26]

There were censorship challenges in a number of states in the US, but they were quickly overturned by the courts. *Ulysses* also encountered censorship problems in New Zealand, where it was initially shown only to audiences segregated by sex, and Australia and South Africa, where it was initially banned. Given the great success of the film in the US and in Britain and Canada, Walter Reade sold a licence to Columbia Pictures for the rest of the world. Columbia consequently made twenty foreign-language versions of the film, but all twenty countries banned the film, and the studio was 'too pusillanimous' to challenge the bans, according to Strick. The culmination of the film's success came with its invitation to compete for a Palme d'Or award at the Cannes Film Festival in 1967. For the French version, Strick subtitled the film with the Valery Larbaud translation, which had been approved by the *Académie Française*, and this copy had been accepted by the Festival. The film's screening was a formal, black-tie affair, well attended, with Strick and his cohort from the film seated in places of honour. But it quickly became apparent that many of the subtitles were obliterated with a grease pencil. Strick tells what happened then:

> I rushed up to the projection room and was confronted by five big men, all in tuxedos. They had been expecting me. In my fractured French I told them that the projection must end. They refused. I flipped the electrical switches and could see, briefly, that the image on the screen had died. The five tuxedoed thugs manhandled me to the door and threw me down the metal steps and a bone in my foot broke. I hobbled onto the stage and announced that the projection was over. The audience protested and what filmmaker can resist the demand of an audience to see his or her film?[27]

However, Strick withdrew the film from the festival.

The most significant and enduring censorship problems encountered by the film of *Ulysses* were those in Ireland, however. There *Ulysses* was refused a certificate by both the censor and the Film Appeals Board. Strick followed the law, which allows a film that had been rejected or cut to be resubmitted for evaluation after seven years, but the film was again rejected by the censors in 1974. 'It was humiliating for me to have this film banned in Ireland', Strick told Michael Dwyer in 2000. Strick returned to Ireland in 2000 to contact the Granary theatre in Cork about staging his production of Aristophanes's *Thesmophoriazusae* and realized he was in a new and different Ireland. He therefore once again submitted his film of *Ulysses* to the Film Appeals Board and this time it was approved without cuts, with a 15 certificate, by the present censor, Seamus Smith. 'Strick Sees *Ulysses* Come Home at Last', read the headline of Michael Dwyer's 11 November 2000 interview with Strick. After a censorship odyssey of thirty-three years, Joseph Strick's film of *Ulysses* was finally shown in Dublin at the dawn of the twenty-first century.

In 1970, Joseph Strick returned to another Grove Press publication of a controversial novel to make a film of Henry Miller's *Tropic of Cancer*. He produced and directed this film, which starred Rip Torn as Henry Miller and Ellen Burstyn as Mona. Henry Miller himself is listed as a 'Spectator' in the credits. In the same year, Joseph Strick won his first Oscar, an Academy Award for Best Documentary Short Subject for his directing of *Interviews with My Lai Veterans*. This documentary was inspired by the work of his daughter, an anthropologist who had spoken to many of the men. In 1979, Strick released his second Joyce film, *A Portrait of the Artist as a Young Man*. Judith Rascoe wrote the screenplay, Betty Botley and Richard Hallinan produced it and Stuart Hetherington did the cinemato-graphy. Stanley Myers once again composed the music (as he had done for *Tropic of Cancer*). Although a new Stephen Dedalus was cast with actor Bosco Hogan, T. P. McKenna (*Ulysses*'s Buck Mulligan) returned to play Simon Dedalus and Maureen Potter (Josie Breen) returned to play Dante Riordan. The film's great triumph was the hellfire and brimstone sermon delivered by Sir John Gielgud. For over forty years Joseph Strick has been making films for the love of it. He told Michael Dwyer in 2000: 'I've always done what I've wanted to do. I thought when I came out of the air force I could do what I liked. I really wanted to be a film director. And here was this gift of life presented to me.'

THE LITERARY CHALLENGES OF *ULYSSES*

To celebrate the end of the twentieth century and usher in the new millennium, Modern Library, a division of the American publishing firm Random House, issued a list of the hundred best novels at the dawn of 2000. The 2003 website[1] juxtaposes the editorial board's list of the top hundred novels of the twentieth century with the readers' list of the top hundred. The board's number one choice for novel of the century was James Joyce's *Ulysses,* which surprised no one – particularly since Random House and Modern Library have been long-time publishers of the novel. The reader's top choices were different but still surprising. Although readers preferred four Ayn Rand novels, three L. Ron Hubbard books, Tolkien's *Lord of the Rings,* Harper Lee's *To Kill a Mockingbird* and George Orwell's *1984* to *Ulysses, Ulysses* still came in a solid number eleven in the readers' poll. These polls inscribe both the challenge and the opportunity Joyce's *Ulysses* offers the filmmaker. On the one hand, the novel is one of the richest, most erudite, most poetic and most difficult pieces of fiction in the English language. On the other hand, it has an irresistible public appeal, largely because its characters and their lives are so recognizably ordinary and human. Can a film of *Ulysses* capture both of these aspects – its status as a literary *tour de force* and its human story of a day in the life of three Irish people living in Dublin in the twentieth century? Put differently, can a film of *Ulysses* add something, offer something *more,* function as a valuable supplement or enhancement to the text for readers and scholars of the novel? At the same time, can it substitute for the novel for those viewers who have never read the book, who possibly will never read the book, or who feel they can't read the book? These challenges to any attempt to film *Ulysses* are so enormous that the first question about filming

Ulysses tends to be whether the attempt should be made at all. In his e-mail interview with the director (31 March 2001), Thom Bennett asked Joseph Strick whether Joyce's work might not be 'unfilmable'. He received this blunt, yet modest, reply:

> To those who say Joyce can't be filmed I just say, 'Don't be ridiculous!' Perhaps someone else will do it better some day but if Joyce worked on film versions who are these bone-heads to say it can't be done? I think I got some of it right. All my movies look full of mistakes to me but every now and then there are moments which I believe are worthy of attention and will be seen for a long time.[2]

Despite the fact that Strick pointedly titled his film *Ulysses by James Joyce* in the opening credits, the question of what his film does and does not accomplish as an adaptation of the novel is none the less legitimate.

The chief difficulty with this question is that it presupposes James Joyce's *Ulysses* to be a stable and identifiable entity, rather than a text whose realization as a piece of writing that is *read* makes it finally a product of interpretation. We might say that each reader *constructs* his or her own *Ulysses*, and that there are as many *Ulysses* (plural) as there are scholars and readers of the text. In practical terms, interpretations vary less with respect to plot and characterization whose understanding has consolidated into a consensus over time than in determining what aspects of the writing are particularly striking or significant – or even revolutionary – given the novel's utter originality in its own time. We might therefore assess the literary challenges to a filming of *Ulysses* by looking at scholarly explorations of Joyce's poetic experimentalism in the novel to determine how and where it resists cinematic translation. Out of many possibilities, three features of the written work can be fruitfully isolated as posing particular difficulties for visualization or cinematic representation, and the third of these deserves exploration at some length. The first is the novel's use of Homer's *Odyssey* as a classical parallel for its exploration of the perils of modern life. This aspect of the novel should be considered both with respect to the importance of the 'mythical method', as T. S. Eliot called it,[3] in early twentieth-century literary Modernism and for its aspiration to the status of a modern *epic*. Second, the novel's ongoing preoccupation with the fate of the artist, and particularly the Irish artist, in the twentieth century poses the challenge of how artistic alienation and artistic development might be represented in film. Third, one might look at what critic Karen Lawrence has called 'the odyssey of style' in Joyce's *Ulysses*,[4] the way the chapters of the novel become increasingly more experimental in their narrative and poetic techniques. Several aspects of this stylistic experimentation are particularly resistant to non-verbal translation: the narrative shifts and changes of perception, the punning and other rhetorical play, and the function of literary parody throughout the work, to name only a few. The aim in looking at these features of the work that have aroused particular scholarly interest over the years is not only to identify the scholarly highlights of the novel's literary interpretation, but also to form a clearer view of the nature of the cinematic challenge they entail.

Joyce's *Ulysses* follows two earlier prose works to which the novel bears both a thematic and a stylistic relationship. After a decade-long struggle with his publisher, Joyce finally, in 1914, published a collection of fifteen short stories entitled *Dubliners*. These stories about the lives of ordinary people living in Dublin in the first few years of the twentieth century are notable for their realism and for their spare, clean, carefully crafted language – a writing Joyce himself called his 'style of scrupulous meanness'. These stories were followed by an autobiographical novel, published in 1916, called *A Portrait of the Artist as a Young Man*, which belongs to the genre of the coming-of-age novel, the *Bildungsroman*, as well as to the novel of artistic development, the *Künstlerroman*. This novel tells the story of young

Stephen Dedalus's struggles against a family life in decline, an oppressive religion and the stifling parochialism of contemporary Ireland. The boy's maturation is narrated in poetic language whose own development throughout the novel imitates Stephen's literacy at various stages of his growth. By the end of the novel, Stephen Dedalus tells a friend, 'When a soul of a man is born in this country there are nets flung at it to hold it back from flight. You talk to me of nationality, language, religion. I shall try to fly by those nets.'[5] With these words he acts out the destiny of his classical name, which recalls Daedalus, the artificer whose son Icarus was equipped with crafted wings to escape from the island of Crete. Icarus soared too close to the sun, which melted their wax and caused him to plunge into the sea and drown. Joyce's *Ulysses*, published in 1922, opens with Stephen Dedalus having returned from Paris and we see him with his wings clipped, as it were, chastened by his failed escape and the impoverished circumstances of his life. Although his mother has died in the interval between *Portrait* and *Ulysses*, we again encounter the Dedalus family, as well as many of the figures we first met in the stories of *Dubliners*. We also encounter the changing and shifting styles of *Portrait* in even more complicated and extreme variations and transmogrifications.

With its title, James Joyce's *Ulysses* signals its relationship to Homer's great post-Trojan War epic, the *Odyssey*,[6] which tells the story of the long, adventurous return of the Greek hero Odysseus after the Trojan War. His journey to rejoin his wife and son and reclaim his kingdom of the island of Ithaca is bedevilled by storm and shipwreck, by the seductions of goddess, sorceress, sirens and narcosis, by hostile natives, cannibals and monsters. During Odysseus's absence, his wife Penelope is beset by suitors who attempt to pressure her into marriage, who threaten to despoil and destroy her palace and who menace her son and servants. The gods finally intervene to set Telemachus, the son of Odysseus, to go in search of his father and to help Odysseus on his dangerous and eventful journey back to his home. This mythological narrative serves to give James Joyce an analogue for a colonized and priest-ridden Ireland, whose most promising young poet, Stephen Dedalus, is threatened with artistic dispossession. Stephen is wracked by guilt for having failed to pray at his mother's deathbed, his drunken father has left the younger children destitute and without care, his friends deride and use him and his artistic society in the Irish Revival excludes him from its circle. Stephen's unconscious journey in search of a spiritual father circuitously leads him to Leopold Bloom, a fallible, humane, smart and courageous Irish advertising canvasser who too is in danger of alienation and dispossession. As a Dublin-born son of a Jewish father and Irish mother, Bloom embarks from a home that is about to be breached by a suitor who will woo his wife Molly during an afternoon tryst. Mourning a lost infant son whose conception burdens him with guilt, Bloom has lost the ability to enjoy conjugal intimacy with his wife and is therefore implicated in her impending infidelity. He must overcome a series of psychological and social obstacles in the course of the day before he can return and once again take possession of his home and the affections of his wife. A key to this successful homecoming is the paternal conjunction of Stephen's quest for a surrogate father and Bloom's quest for a surrogate son. These concurrent journeys take place on a specific day in Dublin: 16 June 1904.

After the publication of *Ulysses* in 1922, Joyce drew up a set of schema for the novel to help mystified friends understand the work's underlying structure. The schema divided the novel into three sections – 'The Telemachiad', 'The Wanderings of Odysseus' and 'Nostos' or 'The Homecoming' – and gave each chapter of *Ulysses* the name of a corresponding Homeric episode. These names have come to serve as chapter titles for Joyce scholars. They correspond to the following pages in the 1986 Gabler edition of James Joyce's *Ulysses* published by Random House:[7]

I. The Telemachiad

> 1. Telemachus (pp. 3–19)
>
> 2. Nestor (pp. 20–30)
>
> 3. Proteus (pp. 31–42)

II. The Wanderings of Odysseus

> 4. Calypso (pp. 45–57)
>
> 5. Lotus-Eaters (pp. 58–71)
>
> 6. Hades (pp. 72–95)
>
> 7. Aeolus (pp. 96–123)
>
> 8. Lestrygonians (pp. 124–150)
>
> 9. Scylla and Charybdis (pp. 151–179)
>
> 10. Wandering Rocks (pp. 180–209)
>
> 11. Sirens (pp. 210–239)
>
> 12. Cyclops (pp. 240–283)
>
> 13. Nausicaa (pp. 284–313)
>
> 14. Oxen of the Sun (pp. 314–349)
>
> 15. Circe (pp. 350–497)

III. Nostos

> 16. Eumaeus (pp. 501–543)
>
> 17. Ithaca (pp. 544–607)
>
> 18. Penelope (pp. 608–644)

The epic dimensions of *Ulysses* should not, in themselves, have posed undue difficulties to the filmmaker, since the epic has been a staple genre of filmmaking since the silent era. We need only remember D. W. Griffith's 1916 silent film *Intolerance* or Abel Ganz's 1927 *Napoleon* to recall how fabulous ancient edifices and the sweep of advancing armies could be captured and enhanced by the cinematographer's lens even in early cinema. The *Odyssey* itself – as a tale of swashbuckling adventure in island settings peopled by monsters, alien peoples and beautiful, seductive women – offers plentiful material for heroic representation to the filmmaker's art. In

1955, the Italian director and screenwriter Mario Camerini made a film version of Homer's *Odyssey*, also translated as *Ulysses*, starring Kirk Douglas, Silvana Mangano and Anthony Quinn. He later went on to work as screenwriter for another cinematic epic, King Vidor's 1956 film of Tolstoy's *War and Peace* starring Audrey Hepburn, Henry Fonda and Mel Ferrer. More recently, the *Odyssey* was turned into a four-hour mini-series by Hallmark Entertainment and American Zoetrope in 1997, and starred Armand Assante as Odysseus, Greta Sacchi as Penelope, Isabella Rossellini as Athena and Vanessa Williams as Calypso. Homer's *Odyssey* is clearly an eminently film-worthy epic. However, this does not mean that Joyce's *Ulysses* is as easily filmed, for Joyce uses the *Odyssey* to very different effect in his novel.

The turn to classical mythology for themes and allusions that inspired early twentieth-century literary Modernism had already infused a diverse set of intellectual disciplines by the late nineteenth century. Friedrich Nietzsche explored the foundations of aesthetics and the arts through the figures of Apollo and Dionysus in *The Birth of Tragedy*. Freud used the analogy of Oedipus to explain the psychoanalytical basis of infantile sexual development, and the Cambridge anthropologists, Jessie Weston and Sir James Frazer, turned to mythology to explore a variety of primitive and folkloric belief systems. In literature, an essay by T. E. Hulme entitled 'Romanticism and Classicism' urged using the discipline of the classics to turn away from the cult of poetic personality and the emotionally indulgent poetic language that characterized Romantic poetry.[8] Classicism became a model for modern poets seeking a renewed commitment to craft, tradition, disciplined writing and impersonality. Classical allusions and analogues consequently abounded in the modern poetry of such Joyce contemporaries as T. S. Eliot, Ezra Pound, H. D. and W. B. Yeats. T. S. Eliot paid the most eloquent tribute to Joyce's use of classical mythology in *Ulysses* when he wrote, 'I hold this book to be the most important expression which the present age has found'.[9] He then went on to explain the function of myth in the novel as nothing less than the transcendence of art over the chaos of the modern world: 'It is simply a way of controlling, of ordering, of giving a shape and a significance to the immense panorama of futility and anarchy which is contemporary history.'[10] One might give homelier descriptions of the use of Homer in Joyce's novel – as the epic domesticated, brought down to domestic and metaphorical residues in the twentieth century. The mighty winds that shipwreck Odysseus and his men are transformed rhetorically in the 'Aeolus' chapter into the hot air of 'windbags' – the overblown oratory of the newspapermen. The spirits of the dead encountered by Odysseus in 'Hades' take the form of memories of dead relatives that are inspired by Bloom's attendance at the funeral of a friend. The one-eyed 'Cyclops', Polyphemus, who gorges himself on Odysseus's men in Homer, is transformed into an Irish nationalist who is a bigot, a man with narrow one-sided or one-eyed views who attacks Bloom, the Jew, with verbal vitriol and an empty Jacob's biscuit tin rather than with rocks (Plate 9). (Strick makes him one-eyed by giving him an eye patch in the film.) And the Odysseus who slays his wife's suitors with his strongbow and arrows is Joyce's wise husband, who overcomes his jealousy at his wife's infidelity by acknowledging his own incrimination in her adultery and by drawing strength from the emotional intimacies of a long marriage to achieve equanimity.

One of the most problematic issues confronting the filmmaker of *Ulysses* concerns the artistic crisis of Stephen Dedalus, whose mythic role as the abandoned son, 'Telemachus', speaks to the specific condition of the modern Irish artist. Stephen's dilemma extends in several directions at once. His drunken father has squandered his birthright and left him without material means. The centuries-long colonization of Ireland by Britain virtually stamped out the native Gaelic language and its culture, leaving the Irish artist with a conqueror's language and a conqueror's poetic traditions for telling his own and his people's story. In *A Portrait of the Artist as a Young Man* Stephen thinks of the British Dean of Studies: 'The language in which we are speaking is his before it is mine. How different are the words *home, Christ, ale, master* on his lips and on mine. I cannot speak or write these words without unrest of spirit. His language, so familiar and so foreign, will always be for me an acquired speech.'[11] That earlier novel also clarifies why neither Irish nationalism nor the cultural Irish Revival, which strikes Stephen as insular and backward-looking rather than progressive, offer him a solution for his artistic paralysis. *Ulysses* offers a number of strategies for Stephen to try, including cribbing from a variety of Irish and English writers such as Oscar Wilde, Douglas Hyde and George Meredith, but Stephen's subtle 'stolen-telling', as plagiarism is called in *Finnegans Wake*, is elusive in *Ulysses* and its significance as an artistic manoeuvre is difficult to pin down. The novel also suggests strategies to avoid, such as the Irish playing the court jester to their British masters, as Joyce believed Wilde had done, and as Buck Mulligan does for the benefit of the Oxford student Haines in the first chapter. Instead Stephen chooses a public forum in which to conduct a psychoanalytical and political critique of the great canonical master of English literature himself, William Shakespeare.

The role of *Hamlet* in *Ulysses* is extremely complex in its illumination of Stephen as a dispossessed son because it places Stephen in a curious relationship with its author, the supreme canonical figure of English literature. The import of the complex analysis Stephen offers in the National Library on Shakespeare's life is best understood as a kind of oedipal manoeuvre, an effort to demythify the Bard. Stephen brings Shakespeare down to the level of realism and restores him to a revisionary history by implicating him in England's expansionist Renaissance imperialism and in an untidy family and public life. Stephen's relationship to his audience of Irish librarians and scholars during this lecture determines what is at stake for him in impressing them and convincing them, but this logic remains elusive and tacit, if significant, in the novel. The clues to its understanding are fleeting and undramatic. We learn that, while his roommate Buck Mulligan and the snobbish Haines, whose father made his money in colonial trade ('He's stinking with money and thinks you're not a gentleman. His old fellow made his tin by selling jalap to Zulus or some bloody swindle or other' [*Ulysses*, p. 6]), are invited to a soirée by the Irish revivalist George Moore, Stephen is pointedly excluded. Stephen's lecture in 'Scylla and Charybdis' is therefore his crucial bid to be taken seriously as an original and erudite mind capable of invigorating the Irish intelligentsia. However, this extended and quirky library lecture would be visually static in a film, with its import for Stephen's situation difficult to convey.[12] The complex relationship Stephen has with the Irish revivalists in the novel takes no clear dramatic form in any scene that could be readily translated into a comprehensible cinematic expression. And the invocations of Shakespeare biographies and their arguable legitimacy as interpretative tools might tax general audiences past the point of illumination even as scholars might have relished their arcane erudition. As a consequence, the film settles for a brief exchange between Stephen and Haines on a possible theological interpretation of *Hamlet*, without implicating Shakespeare in their own Anglo-Irish relationship.

But if Stephen's struggle to achieve artistic and intellectual credibility constitutes a significant aspect of the novel, his author's analogous struggle expresses itself in the very language of the text. This stylistic experimentalism was Joyce's own strategy for finding a unique voice for himself with which to tell the story of Ireland's modernity. The film tackles several of these stylistic challenges, albeit with relatively conventional strategies. Stephen's silent, solitary ruminations as he walks on Sandymount Strand are presented through voice-over narration interpolated with visual images and analogues to his thoughts. Some of the newspaper headlines in 'Aeolus' are offered in the form of wall placards and sandwich boards (Plate 6). And the dry question-and-answer format of the 'Ithaca' chapter that narrates Bloom's and Stephen's return to the Bloom home on Eccles Street is enlivened by the men's enactment of their new friendship in pantomime. One of the film's most concise and hilarious responses to the novel's stylistic play shows Bloom's entry into a filthy eating establishment whose lunchtime customers feed like animals at a trough. Without dialogue or words, the film's sound-track gives us the gulping, snuffling, munching noises of feeding beasts. This is a clever analogue to the 'Lestrygonians' chapter's narration in a kind of gluttonous prose ('swilling, wolfing gobfuls of sloppy food, their eyes bulging, wiping wetted moustaches' [*Ulysses*, p. 138]) – prose that sounds as though it is spoken with one's mouth full when it is read it aloud. But there is, of course, much more to the chapter than this single allusion to the Lestrygonians, who were cannibals in the *Odyssey*. Bloom, who is hungry as lunchtime approaches, meditates not only on food and famine, including the 1846 Irish potato famine, but also on such metaphorical ingestions as the gullibility behind advertising and religion ('Saint Patrick converted him to Christianity. Couldn't swallow it all however' [*Ulysses*, p. 139]). This kind of punning on metaphorical 'swallowing' would be much more difficult to translate to film.

One of the novel's most inventive chapters parallels Odysseus's experience with the friendly Lotus-eaters, who feed lotus blossoms to his sailors. These blooms (with their sly gloss on the name of Leopold Bloom and his pseudonym, Henry Flower) function like a drug that induces such narcosis, languor and bliss that the sailors nearly forget the purpose of their voyage and no longer wish to return home. This chapter of *Ulysses* (episode 5, 'Lotus Eaters') is full of references to spices, flowers, perfumes, the exotic Orient and drugs, as Bloom visits a chemist's shop to order a scented lotion for his wife. How does one convey fragrance and its soothing effects visually in film? In the novel, the prose itself seems sleepy and lazy: 'The far east. Lovely spot it must be: the garden of the world, big lazy leaves to float about on, cactuses, flowery meads, snaky lianas they call them' (*Ulysses*, p. 58). Bloom's thoughts about the sedative effects of religion, prompted by the Roman Catholic Mass and Communion, recall Marx's trope of religion as the opiate of the people. In specific references to the sexual enervation of gelded animals and human eunuchs, the chapter also glosses Bloom's abdication of conjugal responsibility. Bloom's sexual lassitude is exemplified in the last lines of the chapter, by his genitals floating like a lotus blossom in his bath, 'his bush floating, floating hair of the stream around the limp father of thousands, a languid floating flower' (*Ulysses*, p. 71). The film was able to portray Buck Mulligan's stately backside poised to dive into the Forty Foot swimming hole (Plate 2), but the focused frontal genital nudity required to present Bloom's 'limp father of thousands' would have been impossible in a 1967 film, as would reproduction of the delicate lassitude of the prose.

When the prose of the novel functions either imitatively or as parody, these effects intensify resistance to translation into cinematic effects. Four of the most challenging chapters in this respect are 'Sirens', 'Nausicaa', 'Oxen of the Sun', and 'Eumaeus'. 'Sirens', the episode whose Homeric parallel is the lethal seduction of sailors by the

Plate 2. Mulligan

song of maidens on a rock in the sea, allows Joyce to explore the seductions of sentimentality and music. Joyce opens the 'Sirens' chapter with a series of verbal fragments that aspire to the condition of music, like the tuning of an orchestra, as some critics describe it, or an overture that introduces a series of musical motifs. Bloom is characterized by the low sounds of, perhaps, an oboe ('Blew. Blue bloom is on the') while his rival Boylan, in contrast, is announced with tinkling percussion ('Jingle jingle jaunted jingling' [*Ulysses*, p. 210]). Two barmaids, with red and blonde hair, are the 'sirens' of the chapter, and they are characterized both by the colour of their hair ('Bronze by gold') and by their musical laughter. 'Shrill, with deep laughter: after, gold after bronze, they urged each each to peal after peal, ringing in changes, bronzegold, goldbronze, shrilldeep, to laughter after laughter' (*Ulysses*, p. 214). The film offers audible music in this episode, to be sure – a lovely performance of 'Love's Old Sweet Song' – but not the chapter's transformation of its medium into the tonal aspects of music. At the same time, the film eschews an easy translation – the representation of Bloom's highly musical fart. What in the novel's prose sounds like the music of the body – 'prrpffrrppffff' – might have sounded merely like a crass vulgarity on screen. In the 'Nausicaa' chapter Bloom espies some girls playing with young children on the beach and becomes excited by one of the young women, who lifts her skirts and legs in an attempt to see the fireworks overhead. The 'namby-pamby jammy marmalady drawsery' style of the episode, as Joyce called it, presents the indirect description of Gerty MacDowell's thoughts in the precious prose of the ladies' magazine, the novelette, cheap romance fiction, and advertisement. Unlike a singing siren, Gerty seduces with a visual exhibitionism to which the voyeuristic Bloom responds by covertly masturbating. However, the joke on Gerty is that she herself has been seduced by the trash literature she reads, which has infected her thoughts and aspirations with pretentious clichés. The film's cinematic technique makes no attempt to reproduce this intriguing feature of the prose with its self-incriminating critique of popular culture, preferring to give the silent encounter between Bloom and Gerty a stripped visual purity.

'Oxen of the Sun' is set in a maternity hospital, where Bloom hopes to visit a woman in the throes of a difficult childbirth and instead encounters a group of drunken, blasphemous students. In this chapter Joyce parodies human gestation with literary development, by telling the events in evolving styles of English literature from the medieval to the avant-garde. Bloom is introduced in this chapter in Middle English diction, 'Some man that wayfaring was stood by housedoor at night's oncoming. Of Israel's folk was that man that on earth wandering far had fared. Stark ruth of man his errand that him lone led till that house' (*Ulysses*, p. 315). The film makes no attempt to gloss the masterful parodies of literary styles in this chapter, but instead favours keeping its focus on the profanation of reproduction through a series of musical – rather than literary – parodies. In 'Eumaeus', a tired Bloom takes a sleepy Stephen Dedalus to a cabman's shelter for coffee and a biscuit. Joyce narrates this event in what Harry Blamires calls a 'flabby, weary rambling style'[13] that exhibits failed pretensions to elegance. 'For in "Eumaeus", Joyce chooses the "wrong" word as scrupulously as he chooses the right one in the early chapters,' notes Karen Lawrence.[14] How would film translate to the screen a writing that is deliberately, exquisitely bad because it is ineptly trying to be good? Strick's film sets this challenge aside by simply omitting 'Eumaeus.' On the other hand, the film preserves the question-and-answer catechism format of the 'Ithaca' chapter, a chapter which lampoons notions of authority, factuality, certitude and the like by pretending to offer exhaustive truths even while its pronouncements are occasionally misleading, irrelevant and biased. However, instead of a self-betraying catechism, the film's voice-over questions and answers in the Bloom kitchen and garden offer an unsentimental commentary on a pivotal scene of father–son reconciliation whose sentiment remains tacit and confined to a silent, gestural pantomime between the two men.

The film comes closest to the novel's avant-gardism in its rendition of Bloom and Stephen in 'Nighttown', the chapter designated as 'Circe' in the novel. Bloom's sexual fantasies in the 'Circe' chapter are presented in such literally dramatic form – complete with elaborate stage directions and dialogue – that this episode's experimentalism is one of the easiest to transpose to film. Nevertheless, the filmmaker must make choices about the representation of sexually explicit and perverse material on screen. The Odyssean point of the 'Circe' episode, in which the enchantress Circe turns Odysseus's men into swine, is as carefully preserved in the film as in the novel. The spectacle of men transformed into pigs takes on metaphorical meaning in text and film, where decent, ordinary men express and enact gross and unsavoury desires under the influence of the brothel and its madam. Joyce writes in a post-Freudian era in which the polymorphously perverse sexuality repressed by socialization and morality is stripped of much of its pathology and accepted as part of the human libidinal constitution. The film therefore does not shy away from representing Bloom's lechery, masochism and paranoia in the 'Nighttown' section, although it carefully preserves their status as fantasy by cutting deftly between the quotidian tawdry parlour of the brothel and the fantasy locales of Bloom's imaginary enactments. In his aspect as a swine, Bloom snuffles like an animal on all fours (Plate 13) and is ridden like a horse by the masculinized madam, Bella Cohen. But in the film, as in the novel, sex takes place for Bloom only in the imagination, not in Bella Cohen's brothel. And Strick's rendition of Bloom's erotic fantasies is finally much more droll and comically grotesque than erotically pornographic or depraved, a strategy that could be construed as reflecting Bloom's own lack of sophistication – produced by pulp pornography – in formulating his transgressive desires. Inflected by the trash of *Ruby, Pride of the Ring* and *Sweets of Sin*, the erotic imagination of Bloom is shown to be as kitschy in the film as is the romantic imagination of Gerty MacDowell in the novel. When it comes to pornography, Bloom is a rank amateur, we are led to believe by the film. The film even invents mildly risqué covers for Bloom's pornographic reading, although subsequent scholarly research has revealed that *Ruby*, at any rate, turned out to be a circus reform novel by Amye Reade, actually entitled *Ruby. A Novel. Founded on the Life of a Circus Girl*,[15] rather than Victorian pornography.

The avant-garde characteristic of the Joycean text that the film most actively resists, however, is the way the experimentalism of the later chapters of the written text deliberately creates discontinuities and disjunctions that work actively against novelistic coherence. Karen Lawrence recalls early critics, like Joseph Frank, who argued that *Ulysses* developed not in the linear and sequential movement through time that we associate with the novel, but rather in the spatial and non-sequential juxtaposition of elements that we associate with poetry – especially imagist poems.[16] According to Lawrence, the import of this disruption of reader expectations is to transform *Ulysses* into an example of 'anti-fiction', whose point is self-reflexive, to make its own writing the chief drama and focus of the novel.[17] In order to translate this anti-novelistic impulse of the text to cinema, the filmmaker would have to actively foreground play with the conventional techniques of filmmaking in adapting the second half of the novel to film.

Such a strategy could allow a film of *Ulysses* to approximate its generic and stylistic experiments with greater fidelity, but at the price of rupturing viewer investment in character, story and the unfolding of the complex relationships that are the text's most enduring appeal. While Joseph Strick clearly appreciated Joyce's experimentalism and gestures towards it to provocative effect in 'Circe', he nevertheless opted for novelistic coherence, on the one hand, and for a humanistic revelation as the work's outcome, on the other. This is a perfectly legitimate interpretative and aesthetic choice, even if it accommodates the novice and generalist reader of Joyce's work more generously than the modernist scholar and specialist of the twentieth century avant-garde. The challenge of interpretative choices is as great for the filmmaker as it is for the *Ulysses* reader and professional critic of the text. Joseph Strick's film of a contemporary novelistic *Ulysses* set in the 1960s produced a film of considerable relevance to its late-twentieth-century audience. A twenty-first-century film of *Ulysses*, aimed at an audience with postmodern and postcolonial studies as part of its heritage, would need to address the challenges posed by the novel's anti-fictional literary experiments in different ways. In the end, no film can truly be a substitute or proxy for James Joyce's *Ulysses*, but a variety of films can serve as complementary and valuable allies. Joseph Strick's 1967 *Ulysses* clearly offered a post-World War II audience a splendid illumination of Joyce's literary masterpiece.

4

ULYSSES IN A CINEMATIC MEDIUM

The opening title of Joseph Strick's film of *Ulysses* makes it clear that this film is inextricably linked to Joyce's novel: 'Ulysses by James Joyce', it reads, printed in a style of type that imitates the covers of early editions of the work. The pledge in the film's title carries with it its complex responsibility to a dual audience. Joseph Strick himself articulated this challenge to Stephen Watts when he said: 'Our obligation is to make a film good enough for people who have read the book. Our opportunity is to create an entirely new experience for those who have not.'[1] Yet the task of scripting an adaptation – which, wherever possible, Strick and co-screenwriter Fred Haines rigorously limited to Joyce's own words – does not preclude that singular stamp of creativity or artistic vision that twentieth-century film criticism captured in the term *auteur*. I introduce the term only to suggest that Joseph Strick's direction of *Ulysses* complicates his fidelity to the text with interpretative and inventive enhancements that produce a singular vision of the novel. Audiences and scholars are clearly divided in their response to that vision, with scholars demanding that the cinematic supplement adequately compensate for everything a film of *Ulysses* must leave out. Richard Ellmann, for one, remained dissatisfied with the film's intellectual economy. 'The film is not without conscience', he wrote, 'but it has no innovations commensurate with those of its original'.[2] But at the time of its release, film critics largely praised the film's aesthetic achievement, which the renowned critic Judith Crist called 'A Superb Screen Translation of Joyce's "Ulysses"' in the headline of her review. She went on to pay a majestic tribute to this translation when she wrote, 'Like its source, Joseph Strick's film has classic scope, a grandeur and a throbbing humanism, an intense dramatic power and a wild and unrestrained wit, a lyric beauty and a wild, robust humor.'³ The difference between Ellmann's and Crist's judgements turns on an interpretative crux – namely, whether *Ulysses* is to be valued for its enactment of an extremity of human intelligence or for its affectionate embrace of the complexity of human ordinariness. The film's humanism – denigrated by Ellmann as a diminution ('The epic contracts into a domestic comedy') – is none the less a legitimate and insightful interpretation of the novel, as Joyce's own words endorse. Joyce told Arthur Power that 'an author must not write for the arty'. He went on to argue that the modern mind 'is interested above all in subtleties, equivocations, and the subterranean complexities which dominate the average man and compose his life'.⁴ Joseph Strick's film of *Ulysses* celebrates these complexities, I believe, and the filmmaking process that shaped this humanistic vision can be appreciated as a gifted confrontation with its creative challenges.

To this end, I hope to track three major manoeuvres by the film which illuminate the logic of its selections and emphases. First, the film gives primacy to the intertwined family theme. This requires the cinematic version to tighten and reorganize the novel's narrative to make the complex triangular relationship between Stephen Dedalus, Leopold Bloom and Molly Bloom intelligible, coherent and meaningful. The script therefore highlights the role of Bloom's guilt and grief over the death of his son Rudy in producing the impotence that triggers Molly's adultery with Blazes Boylan. Bloom's mourning, in turn, parallels the crippling effects of Stephen's guilt and grief at his mother's death, which impairs his artistic self-realization. Their encounter at the end of the story, restoring parental warmth to Stephen and the ability to parent to Bloom, provides the healing outcome of Bloom's anxious day that allows him to survive and even triumph over Molly's infidelity, an outcome that her lyrical night-time monologue validates. Second, the film connects the domestic plot of imperilled family life to the political theme of alienation and extrusion produced by the British and Irish anti-Semitism that conditions Bloom's isolation in the city in which he was born. By setting the film in contemporary (1960s) post-revolutionary Ireland, the film lets a more universal anti-Semitism, imbued with the urgencies of the World War II realization of its consequences, stand in for British imperialism as a salient oppression. Third, the film offers an array of visual techniques to foreground the affective or emotional interior lives of the figures – those 'subterranean complexities which dominate the average man' that Joyce mentioned to Arthur Power. Together these three strategies preserve the major contours of the Odyssean parallel: the fragmented family, the perilous voyage in alien lands, and the courage and wit required to survive these conditions. With them, Joseph Strick produces a cinematic interpretation of the novel that is intensely humanistic, offering an ironic and occasionally transgressive vision that sees the world, for all its perils, as ultimately benign and comic.

The film, like the book, opens with Buck Mulligan shaving on the circular turret of the Martello tower, where the witty and noisy T. P. McKenna fills the scene with a colourful quickness that offsets the restrained, stiff, dark figure of the brooding Maurice Roëves. Roëves plays a gentler, sweeter Stephen Dedalus than the one Bosco Hogan offers in Strick's 1979 *A Portrait of the Artist as a Young Man* – a difference that may make Hogan's portrayal conform more closely to readers' expectations for the role.[5] The film, however, brings to the surface some of the sweetness that is hidden and interiorized behind Stephen's acrid and haughty demeanour in the novel, and thereby makes his affinities with Bloom more plausible, if less ironic. These affinities are further reinforced through the selections and emphases of the film's first three scenes, which rearrange the novel's 'Telemachiad'. The Martello tower scene is dominated by Stephen's nightmare memory of refusing to kneel at his mother's deathbed, conveyed in a flashback that uses a bowl of spilled bile or vomit as a potent objective correlative for Stephen's repulsion by the dying woman's disease and decay. In the film, the bowl falls twice with a clank, first in the flashback and then again in the turret, when Stephen knocks Mulligan's shaving bowl off the parapet and splashes his leg with an imagined corruption. The spilling of the bowl is a cinematic invention – for it never falls in the novel, neither at the deathbed nor in the Martello tower. Before moving on to Stephen's teaching in Dalkey, the film follows 'Telemachus' with 'Calypso' in order to juxtapose the dour, theatrical breakfast presided over by Mulligan in the tower with the cosy conjugal breakfast in bed at 7 Eccles Street. Milo O'Shea as Bloom is never more charming than in his opening scenes, when he trundles the rattling tray up the stairs, opens curtains and windows, pretends to model Molly's bra and panties (Plate 3) and then sits comfortably on the bed with her to explain 'metempsychosis' (Plate 4). Barbara Jefford's smile when she reads Boylan's note and tells Bloom about it, together with the flash-forward to the romping Boylan hurling himself on Molly in that very bed, prepares us for her complex emotions at the end of the day. But it also links the foreshadowed adultery to its remote cause, when Milo O'Shea – explaining 'metempsychosis' as the transmigration of souls – looks with melancholy at a photograph of a crying newborn baby. The photograph is a cinematic invention that wordlessly introduces the dead infant that is the fulcrum of the family plot.

Plate 3. Bloom modelling Molly's underwear.

Plate 4. Molly and Bloom in the bedroom.

This first image of Rudy prompts the cut back to Stephen, now teaching at his Dalkey school, and preparing to help a sad, dull little boy with his sums. Here the film preserves one of Stephen's kindliest moments – his silent, haunting paean to maternal tenderness, delivered in a paternal posture towards the boy that foreshadows the images of a paternal Bloom with his fantasy son, and with Stephen himself at the end of the film. A little later in the funeral carriage, the sight of Stephen Dedalus by his father ('Full of his son') triggers Bloom's melancholy over *his* dead son. A series of fantasies of Rudy as a boy now amplify Bloom's sketchy thoughts in the novel: 'If little

Rudy had lived. See him grow up. Hear his voice in the house. Walking beside Molly in an Eton suit. My son. Me in his eyes' (*Ulysses*, p. 73). We see a serious, dark-haired little boy looking at ducks in a pond with his mother and then playing chess with his delighted father in the family kitchen, two broadly striped mugs before them. When these mugs recur later in the film, we see Bloom and Stephen in the same kitchen (Plate 18), in the exact position Bloom and Rudy had occupied in the fantasy, with the striped mugs now holding their cocoa. The film offers in its version of the homecoming ('Ithaca') a far less equivocal and more positive resolution of the familial crisis than is offered by the novel. Beginning with the end of the Nighttown sequence, where Bloom is pointedly posed like a *Pietà* with an unconscious Stephen in his arms, the logic of the visual images suggests that, having embraced the loss of his son, Bloom can now enjoy his resurrection and restoration. In the warmth and congeniality of the kitchen scene, more is conveyed by smiles and gestures than by the information the voice-over narration offers in its catechism format. Bloom now teaches Stephen the Hebrew script he might once have taught Rudy, and his demonstration of the thumbed nose suggests that he even shares with Stephen his triumph over the anti-Semitic Citizen. This simultaneous resolution of Bloom's paternal and racial crisis is much neater than the novel's, which is clouded by Stephen's tactless and puzzling rendition to Bloom of a nasty song about little Harry Hughes who is decapitated by a Jew's daughter (*Ulysses*, pp. 565–567). By unceremoniously dumping Boylan's empty fruit basket in the rubbish bin (another cinematic invention), Bloom also signals his triumph over his wife's adultery. And the film's most far-reaching invention even offers a made-up resolution for Stephen's lovelessness, when, on his departure from Eccles Street, we see him meeting a young woman and walking with her. As though in an Oedipal gender revision, Stephen has killed his mother back in 'Nighttown' and, by reclaiming a father, is now free to love. This invented scene patently violates the novel's

Plate 5.   Stephen on Sandymount Strand.

ambiguity about Stephen's future, although it uncannily looks forward to the visual image of a cinematic James Joyce (Ewan McGregor) walking the streets of Dublin with Nora Barnacle (Susan Lynch) in the 1999 Pat Murphy film based on Brenda Maddox's *Nora*.

Bloom's introduction into the film as a Jew is accomplished by two cleverly ironic transitions. The first occurs in front of the Martello tower, when the Englishman Haines – played with toothy and vapid hauteur by Graham Lines – diverts Stephen from taking up the touchy relations of Britain and Ireland by declaring: 'I don't want my country to fall into the hands of the Jews'. The scene segues into the kitchen of Leopold Bloom, who, with his apron, cat and breakfast tray, looks a highly unlikely threat to the United Kingdom. This manoeuvre is repeated again at the end of 'Nestor', when Mr Deasy, the school's headmaster, delivers the punch line of his joke to Stephen (that the Irish never persecuted the Jews because they never let them in). The film here again cuts back to Bloom, by a store window emblazoned with a Star of David, his identity intensified with Semitic music. Without a word, the shift renders Deasy's joke doubly ironic, because there are, as we see, Irish Jews after all, and because they suffer, if not persecution, then certainly prejudice like Deasy's. But

Plate 6. The pressroom.

even though anti-Semitism is the film's central political focus, Strick follows the novel's deft handling of its consequences for Bloom's daily life by clarifying that not all of Bloom's setbacks are produced by bigotry, nor is Bloom a passive victim when they are. The film carefully averts the melodramatic with the comic when showing Bloom responding with dignity and courage to dismissal, derision or abuse in his public life. The squalls in the newspaper office preserve the windiness of the 'Aeolus' episode, with its clanking presses, rustling papers and rhetorical flourishes, while using, to Brechtian effect, wall placards ('You Can Do It', 'Ecce Homo') that simulate the capitalized newspaper headlines of the novel.[6] Their choices are not arbitrary, pointing as they do to Stephen's frustrations and Bloom's psychological buffeting. Bloom's efforts to secure the Keyes advertisement are rebuffed both verbally and visually with Miles Crawford's K.M.A. and K.M.R.I.A. ('kiss my royal Irish arse') uttered and carried on sandwich-boards by the scurrying newsboys. The film, like the novel, here plays with its own artifice as well as with its own visual character.

Later in the pub, the K.M.A. is reprised and reversed as the outcome of the showdown between Bloom and the Citizen with his cyclopian eye-patch. In his finest performance in the film, Milo

O'Shea's vulnerability in the face of truculent questions ('What is your nation, if I may ask?') is countered both with his indignant claim to citizenship ('Ireland. I was born here. Ireland.') and his refusal to evade his Jewishness. The escalating verbal violence is coded with anti-Semitic slurs ('that sheeny', 'gone around to collect the shekels') and reinforced with a post-World War II gloss by having the mongrel Garryowen of the novel replaced with an aggressive German shepherd lunging after the escaping Bloom in his chariot of a convertible.[7] As Bloom triumphantly returns his own K.M.A. to the Citizen with a rude gesture (Plate 8) and a juvenile stuck-out tongue,

Plate 7.   Bloom and Mulligan at the Museum.

Plate 8. Bloom triumphant.

the film perfectly captures the explosion of violence into the comic, mock-heroic climax of the last sentence of the 'Cyclops' chapter: 'And they beheld Him even Him, ben Bloom Elijah, amid clouds of angels ascend to the glory of the brightness at an angle of fortyfive degrees over Donohoe's in Little Green street like a shot off a shovel.'[8]

Bloom's other psychological peril – his wife's impending adultery with Blazes Boylan – is less easily conquered, however. The film cleverly exploits the novel's preoccupation with modern advertisement – and Bloom's attention to it as an advertising canvasser – by promoting the face of Boylan on posters and billboards,[9] thereby glossing Boylan's jobs as concert promoter and 'billsticker', as Bloom pejoratively thinks of him. Boylan turns up everywhere like a bad penny. When Bloom passes the shop window of a business called 'Boylan', a female mannequin with a resemblance to Molly triggers a flashback to the débâcle of Rudy's conception, prompted by her lusty 'Give us a touch, Poldy. God, I'm dying for it.' The juxtaposition implicitly links Bloom's guilt and impotence following Rudy's death to his wife's impending sexual affair that for Bloom has public as well as private consequences. The embarrassment he fears becomes externalized when Boylan's entering the pub with his trysting gift of a fruit basket on his arm cues an impudent cuckoo clock to pronounce Bloom a 'cuckold, cuckold, cuckold'. The film indicates this complicated dynamic of guilt, desire and anxiety virtually wordlessly, with no exposition, conveyed chiefly through cuts, shifts and juxtapositions of images and scenes.

In the film, as in the novel, both Molly and Boylan's adultery and the scenes of the Blooms in love are events experienced in the mind. Arguably the film's greatest challenge was the invention of devices for representing the vast amount of interior experience offered by the book. The film's reviewers generally praised its strategies for

Plate 9. The Citizen hurling a biscuit tin.

representing pure thought. Richard Coe writes: 'The cinematic style is analogous to that of the novel, the visual world an obbligato to interior thoughts, seemingly so vagrant yet logical to these particular individuals. The cutting in and out is abrupt as it is in Joyce and the perpetual streak-of-consciousness [*sic*] flows on and on.'[10] In addition to such conventional devices as flashbacks and voice-over narration, the film invented an array of tactics for filling the screen with visual images suggested by the verbalized thoughts – particularly in 'Nighttown' and during Molly Bloom's soliloquy. Even earlier, the film announces its refusal to back away from these challenges. The 'Proteus' chapter of *Ulysses* is virtually silent and is populated chiefly by the single figure of Stephen Dedalus meditating on a variety of subjects while ambling along Sandymount Strand (Plate 5). The sequence quite refutes Richard Ellmann's complaint about the film that 'Instead of expurgating the body, it expurgates the mind. Masturbation is in, cogitation is out.'[11] Indeed, Ray Loynd calls this section of the film its 'most lyrical soliloquy'.[12] The film even manages to preserve one of the episode's most arresting and anomalous narrative manoeuvres – a second-person narration. Asking himself whether he would save a man from drowning, Stephen carries on a dialogue with himself: 'Would you do what he did? . . . The truth, spit it out. I would want to. I would try. I am not a strong swimmer. Water, cold soft.' Stephen's ponderous opening meditation on the 'Ineluctable modality of the visible' is lightened by the film's self-reflexive play. When Stephen closes his eyes, the screen goes black, obliging the viewer momentarily to *not-see* with Stephen, making us *film-blind* like the mock-blind Stephen tapping the ground with his ashplant cane.

The earlier scene of Stephen as teacher in the Dalkey school omits his lessons on Pyrrhus's resistance to the Romans and John Milton's 'Lycidas' but does give a visual gloss to some of the intellectual preoccupations in the novel – although those of Bloom rather than those of Stephen. In the novel, Bloom recalls a mnemonic device for remembering the colours of the rainbow that he was taught in school: 'Roygbiv Vance taught us: red, orange, yellow, green, blue, indigo, violet' (*Ulysses*, p. 308). Bloom's teacher, Vance, had also taught him 'Thirty-two feet per second. Law of falling bodies' and in one of his 'Nighttown' fantasies Bloom remembers these two physical facts together as a unit – 'Roygbiv. 32 feet per second' (*Ulysses*, p. 397). Strick's film transposes this bit of teaching to Stephen Dedalus in Dalkey, chalking the formulae on the blackboard behind Stephen along with the word 'Cod'. Readers familiar with the novel recognize these as codes for bits of information or facts that unfold into significant little themes in *Ulysses* with a curious afterlife in Joyce's *Finnegans Wake*. In this later text the *fall*, and falling objects, as well as the colours of the rainbow play significant roles as recurring motifs of sin and redemption. In the film of *Ulysses*, Strick leaves 'Roygbiv. 32 feet per second' attached to the classroom, but allows it to recrudesce in Molly's fantasy, when she lampoons Bloom's pedantry with a fantasy of her husband in a professorial mortar board, holding forth on ROYGBIV and 32 feet per second before a blackboard. These small verbal allusions may be inadequate to register Bloom's lively curiosity and practical intelligence on many subjects, including physics, to the novice viewer, but they none the less serve as a small signal to readers familiar with the novel to let them know that the film is not oblivious to the text's minor intellectual preoccupations. And the incongruous 'Cod' – recalling the 'deadhand' in 'Nighttown' declaring that 'Bloom is a cod' (*Ulysses*, p. 404) – reminds us that *Ulysses*, in both text and film, deflates its own pedantries and intellectual pretensions.

However, both novel and film also take aesthetic issues more seriously. On Sandymount Strand, Stephen's abstract musings on human genesis are pictured with abstract, but suggestive, shapes and images: beautiful figures of pure curves and ancient fertility sculptures. This long, lovely sequence with its poetic photography of sunlit sand and sea and its chaste visual analogues for Stephen's

Plate 10. Stephen at the maternity hospital.

sensitive meditations on reproduction contrasts with the later
bawdiness of 'Oxen of the Sun', set in the student lounge of the
maternity hospital. Backed by the skeletons and charts of medical
pedagogy (Plate 10), the abstruse conversations of the interns and
their friends are displaced onto a series of dirty ditties that articulate
the theme of Homeric 'crimes against fecundity' committed when
Odysseus's men slay the sun god's sacred fertility oxen. Mulligan sings
his profanation of sexuality as a series of mock-shocking family plaints
– 'Cousin Caspar's been transpo-orted for a homo-secks-oo-al
crrrrime/And my sister has abo-orted for the forty-second time'. And

Plate 11. Bloom in the dungeon.

Stephen, introduced by Mulligan as a 'priestified bard', sounds a Latinate chant – a traditional altar boy parody, according to Strick – that rhymes *deitas* with 'Stick it up your ass'. The film's shift from literary parody to musical parody in this episode marks one of its most radical inventions, with a substantial departure from Joyce's text. Joyce scholars differ sharply on its result. Richard Ellmann complains that 'the medical students in the lying-in hospital are rowdy boys rather than lewd scholars, and sing bawdy catches instead of talking'. But Richard M. Kain's review of the film in the *James Joyce Quarterly*

Plate 12. Bloom with Bello.

calls the scene 'a marvelously roistering atmosphere dominated by Mulligan, who renders a surgical ballad with references to operations, castrations, amputations in the gallows humor of "Johnny, I Hardly Knew Ye".[13]

The naughty discourse of 'Oxen' is turned inside out in 'Circe', where the Strick film takes up Joyce's scripting of the brothel episode in the form of an Expressionist drama. Expressionism collapses the boundaries between inner and outer, between mind and phenomena, with the result that Bloom's most intimate libidinal and social fantasies are acted out in grotesque and distorted scenarios of the soul. By carefully following the sequence of the novel's 'Circe' chapter, the film's 'Nighttown' sequence preserves the myriad scenes that show Bloom to be a man of infinite variety – a spiritual human circus[14] troped by the theatricality of a central circus ring and patent burlesques. His soft-shoe routine with Josie Breen is delightful, and his accusation by a feisty Mary Driscoll armed with bucket and scouring brush and betrayed by her accent ('with a request for a saya-fe-ty-pin') is wonderfully farcical. In the film's interpretation, Bloom's most secret fantasies, desires and feelings of guilt are droll rather than perverse or particularly shameful or painful. Bosley Crowther notes that the film's rendition of the brothel fantasy's 'weird and symbolistic rites is every bit as meaningful and brilliant as a similar passage in Frederico Fellini's *8½*.'[15] But Bloom as masochist, tricked out like a fat girl in dowdy nightgown, untidy wig and curlers (Plate 12), looks ridiculous and sounds silly rather than pornographic. The joke of his humiliation ('I love the danger') is its lame eroticism. This may explain why critics quite willing to express shock at Molly Bloom's four-letter words in the film[16] appeared completely unfazed by the potentially far

Plate 13. The humiliation of Bloom.

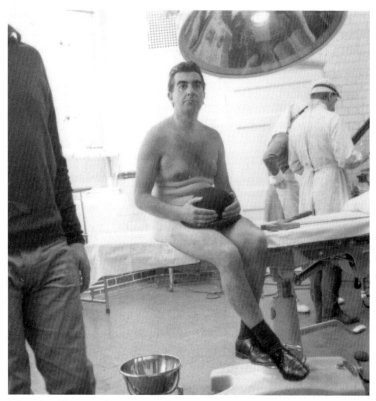

Plate 14. Bloom in the operating theatre.

greater perversity of Bloom's transsexual masochism. The patent theatricality throughout the 'Nighttown' episode has transformed the *outré* sexuality into a mocking register, as it does in the novel. The Middle Eastern Bloom in fez and caftan, lounging with his odalisque, or impersonating Valentino's Sheik, broadly acts out clichés of oriental voluptuousness. Bloom's political fantasies similarly preserve their mock-ideology from the novel when brought to the screen. Bloom speechifying in his working-class overalls and cap (Plate 15) to the stirring rhythms of the communist 'Internationale' is as theatrically absurd as the homage tendered him as emperor ('God save Leopold the First!' 'Little Father! Little Father!'). His range of political successes, from acclaim as the world's greatest reformer to the founder of the new Bloomusalem[17] offers farcical wish-fulfillment of Bloom's political blather in 'Cyclops', culminating in the raising of the standard of Zion. By remaining close to the text here, the film preserves the wild vacillations of power or prestige that underlie Bloom's highest and lowest moments in 'Nighttown'. But, given the time of the filming in the 1960s, little more than a decade after the McCarthy era's notorious 'Red-baiting' in the United States, Bloom's socialist aspirations and paranoid fears of denunciation and

Plate 15. Bloom addressing the workers.

persecution also offer a more serious gloss on the film's recent contemporary political moment.

The final nadir of Bloom's 'Nighttown' experiences is his absurd adultery fantasy, in which he acts as his rival's lackey, decked out in livery, wig and cuckold's horns that serve as Boylan's hat-rack. The scene follows the novel in censoring what Bloom sees through the keyhole, but, as in the novel, the implication is that with this fantasy Bloom has confronted (and implicitly conquered) the dreaded fear that has haunted him all day. The film suggests this resolution even more strongly than the novel by showing a self-possessed and even bossy Bloom returning home to clear the violated bedroom of its messy underclothes and things before climbing into bed, at the opposite end, with his wife Molly, at the end of his day. The film further manoeuvres the marital resolution structurally, by giving Bloom and Molly reciprocal and congruent memories of their first lovemaking on Howth Head. Because Martha Clifford has no visual presence in the novel, Joseph Strick excises her from the film altogether, letting Bloom's excitation by Gerty MacDowell alone stand in for his oblique infidelities to Molly. This frees the film to replace the song from Von Flotow's *Martha* in 'Sirens' ('M'appari') with Simon Dedalus singing 'Love's Old Sweet Song'. Bloom, sipping his glass of burgundy and eating his sandwich, is reminded by the melody of the day on Howth Head, when he and Molly shared a seedcake in a kiss. The logic of the oral trigger of a memory of oral pleasure is preserved, and the strategic depiction of Bloom's intensely significant attachment to the memory clarifies poignantly what the appearance in the pub of the jaunty Boylan with his gift basket places at risk. The film also stays with the novel's pointed siding with Molly Bloom against the family-destroying masculinism of Dublin's pub culture. Bloom's greater decencies ('he has sense enough not to squander every penny piece he earns down their gullets and looks after his wife and family', Molly thinks in bed [*Ulysses*, p. 636]) are defended against the snide innuendoes and belittlement of the drinking men.[18] The film's visual and narrative reinforcement of the Howth memory, which recurs at the end of Molly's night-time thoughts, frames both of the Blooms' various infidelities and provides the tacit explanation for how their marriage might survive adultery.

Early in her soliloquy Molly pronounces her adultery as 'anyhow its done now once and for all' and explicitly privileges her Howth day with Bloom when she says 'its only the first time after that its just the ordinary do it and think no more about it'. Of course, she not only thinks a great deal about it, she also remembers, relives and relishes her afternoon with Boylan and her memories of Gardner (whom the film conflates with Mulvey), her erotic fantasies, and all the voluptuous longings in her life. As in its version of 'Circe', the film supplements the lyrical voice of 'Penelope' with suggestive images and scenes. Here, more than elsewhere in the film, we see what Ray Loynd in his review sees as the film's most 'literary' aspect: 'the camera is constantly on a mission to find the visual image appropriate to the words'.[19] Bloom's ordered breakfast eggs, both cooked and smashed, recur as both domestic and reproductive symbols. The lovemaking with Boylan is replayed in a great variety of kisses and gambols, sometimes underlined with erotic sculptures that Richard Kain identifies as 'the *mithuna* figures of the Indian and Malay peninsulas'.[20] And Molly's pleasure in the male body conjures up young men diving and a great deal of classical marble statuary – at one point farcically acted out by Boylan posing with a fig leaf. Molly's thoughts of Bloom veer either towards the jealous (Bloom glancing at Mary Driscoll or surrounded by admiring ladies) or to the comically vindictive (pouring tea on Bloom's sputtering head in revenge for his breakfast request; giving him a bicycle spill for ogling a young woman). A number of critics have remarked on the range of emotional and poetic registers with which Barbara Jefford's performance of Molly plays out what critic Louis Cook calls 'the entire glorious and unsanitary business of lovemaking' in her thoughts.[21] Richard Coe of the *Washington Post* writes:

> As she goes back in her memory to her meeting with Bloom, the death of their son, her recollection of Gibraltar and her British lover, of singing 'Love's Old Sweet Song' on tacky concert stages, of sexual experiences and of sexual non-experiences, a double character is created. In the one she is the cantankerous, life-loving voluptuary, in the second she is Joyce, pouring out thoughts and knowledge from a rich, allusive mind. This is a *tour de force* of glittering brilliance.[22]

Molly Bloom's soliloquy, which ends the film with twenty minutes of lyrical prose, inevitably stimulated conflicting responses in critics and viewers. Some of the comments remind us that 1967 was barely at the genesis of what became known as 'the second feminist movement', a relatively dark age when frank sexual thoughts and desires were particularly troublesome if they were uttered on screen by a woman. Clifford Terry of the *Chicago Tribune*, for example, says of the soliloquy, 'Those not familiar with the book may regard it as one woman's crudity-catharsis',[23] and Bosley Crowther calls Molly 'a woman who is clearly over-sexed'.[24] But Judith Crist, in contrast, calls Molly's screen soliloquy 'a unique revelation of female sexology'.[25] Compared to the literary criticism on Molly Bloom at the time,[26] the film critics offer a far more generous and positive response to her character – a tribute to both Strick's complex and nuanced interpretation of Molly and the textured performance by Barbara Jefford. Thus we find some critics surprised by an entirely different aspect of the woman in the film. Richard Kain writes, 'And Molly! What a splendid creature she is, though no doubt much prettier and more refined than we had expected. Her words are shocking, beyond doubt, yet Barbara Jefford's reading invests the soliloquy with a deep ground-swell of poetry.'[27] And Charles Champlin was slightly disappointed in the portrayal of Molly because she seemed to him 'a shade too intellectual, a shade too little the earthy sensualist I had expected'.[28] Joseph Strick's efforts to structure Molly's portrayal in a series of contrapuntal images that balance her different aspects and moods is clearly validated by this varied critical response. The Molly tumbling in bed with Boylan at one moment has artistic and social aspirations in another, and it is the art of Barbara Jefford that, no matter how bawdy her thoughts, how fatuous her vanities, how rude her opinions, her Molly is somehow imbued with an enduring dignity. The film reinforces this by showing us more images than the novel of a Molly imagining herself as smartly dressed and about in society, a diva on stage, an elegant matron in the tearoom, an authoress signing her book for admiring ladies. The novel's Molly Bloom does have intellectual desires, though they chiefly veer off into costumes and postures: 'Id love to have a long talk with an intelligent welleducated person Id have to get a nice pair of red slippers like those Turks with fez used to sell', she thinks (*Ulysses*, p. 641). The film cleverly replaces the slippers with the wonderfully sweeping, feathery eyeglass frames its Molly chooses because they make her *look* intellectual. And the film's fantasies of Molly in bed with the professorial Stephen, reading with the absurd spectacles that turn even a chaste kiss into a poke in his eye, offer a cinematic invention that shows that Molly is different women for different men. This nicely captures the theatrical in the sexual roles Molly Bloom plays, as Kimberly Devlin argues in her essay: 'Theatricality is also heavily embedded in Molly's sexual fantasies focused on Stephen.'[29]

The film succeeds in making Molly Bloom not a sex object, but a sex subject in our contemporary sense of that term – that is, a thinking agent who has her own vision of the world with her own views on men, women, sex and gender roles. Sometimes she gets things wrong. When she wonders why Bloom showed Stephen her photograph ('what is he driving at now showing him my photo'), she imagines them leering and guffawing in the kitchen, when the film had earlier shown us Bloom's pride and Stephen's nonplussed and uncomfortable response. When she is at her most candid, dreaming about the delights of fellatio, she is also at her most wistful, regretting that one had best forego the pleasure because 'that's what gives the women the moustaches'. William Glackin was most greatly moved not by the soliloquy's sexuality, but by the pathos of such lines as 'I wish somebody would write me a loveletter . . . true or not it could fill up your whole day'.[30] In spite of her fantasies, the screen Molly also reflects on sex in the real world, practised by real people who are difficult to imagine as sexual at all. We see her mind's eye transforming the fertile Methodist, Theodore Purefoy, into a corpulent man munching something from a box with bovine satisfaction, juxtaposed with the image of a toddler in winter clothes looking like a real child. Sex begets (or fails to beget, as the Blooms are painfully aware) children and responsibilities. And a hilariously rumpled and desiccated old couple is juxtaposed (and exposed) with Molly's verbal image of the Mastianskys' sex life ('better put it into me from behind the way Mrs Mastiansky told me her husband made her like the dogs do it'). Sex, Molly Bloom knows, is not just for the young and the restless. But neither does she forget what it was like when she herself was young, and in the end Molly's memories return to Gibraltar, with its winding narrow streets and the Barbary apes with their young on the high cliffs, and walking with Gardner. And as the scene of young love in Gibraltar oscillates with the memory of Howth Head, it is finally Bloom who stirs her most intensely romantic memory. The film ends with a rare film image of a woman's face straining and dissolving at the moment of orgasm, a visual reflection of the climactic verbal 'yes' with which Molly Bloom and the film affirm the joy of life.

Joseph's Strick's film of James Joyce's *Ulysses* may not yet have attained the settled critical judgement it deserves as a film in its own right. Academic criticism of the film has been surprisingly scant and – with the exception of Richard Kain's very supportive 1967 review in the *James Joyce Quarterly* – surprisingly negative. Richard Ellmann's sharp criticism in his *New York Review of Books* article has already been noted. Alan Spiegel alludes to it only with a few words as a 'bad film'

– 'flat, pedestrian, and uncinematic' – while Edward Murray calls it 'mediocre' after giving it a condescending 'A for effort' and conceding that 'The attempt to make a movie version of *Ulysses* was doomed to failure'. Three further books on film and fiction by Joyce critics (Morris Beja, Richard Pearce and Thomas Burkdall) mention the film, barely, if at all.[31] How does one reconcile this tepid notice from the academy with the overwhelmingly superlative notices the film received during its initial opening in the spring of 1967? One can certainly find evidence of reviewer ignorance of the Joycean text, with the funniest 'bloomer', as Paul Van Caspel might call it, being the *Berkeley Daily Gazette* reviewer's identification of Leopold Bloom as 'a dental surgeon'.[32] But this is rare, and most reviewers appear to have a sharp and detailed grasp of the novel's text and its relation to the film. It may also be that reviewers bent over backwards in their praise to pre-empt and forestall any censorship problems the film might have encountered in the United States. But the likeliest explanation may point to a different historical development, one that allowed the film to be eclipsed by the burgeoning European, American and Japanese art film production of the later twentieth century, while Joyce's *Ulysses* rose to become the undisputed universal gold standard of fiction. It is therefore important to remember that, at the time of its release, Joseph Strick's film was considered a masterpiece that would endure as 'one of the great motion pictures', as Louis Cook of the *Detroit Free Press* called it. 'It will stand alongside "Children of Paradise," "The Great Illusion," and "Two Women",' he wrote. Charles Champlin of the *Los Angeles Times* called it 'a remarkable achievement, a further chapter in the maturity of film'. And Robert Sullivan of the *Capital Times* predicted that 'It will undoubtedly be accepted as one of the great classics of cinematic art.'[33] They may not have been vindicated in their predictions, but perhaps their judgements deserve a renewed consideration in the twenty-first century.

5

JOSEPH STRICK'S *ULYSSES*, IRELAND AND DUBLIN

James Joyce wrote *Ulysses* as an epic of a modern European capital that would put Ireland, and Dublin, before the world in the complexity of both its history and its modernity. Although he wrote the novel during the years which saw Ireland fighting for its independence from Britain, Joyce set *Ulysses* in 1904, at a time when the scandal and ensuing death of Parnell had made the prospect of a Free State unlikely and unpromising in the near future. In contrast, Joseph Strick set the film of *Ulysses* not at the time of the novel, in 1904, but in the contemporary decade in which it was filmed: the 1960s, when Ireland was already a republic, albeit divided, with its northern counties retained as part of the United Kingdom. But by updating its historical moment, the cinematic version of *Ulysses* lost its ability to represent the anomalous situation of a twentieth-century European capital that was simultaneously an unwilling British colony.[1] James Fairhall illuminates what this means in practical terms when he writes, 'Legally, in 1904, Leopold Bloom is every bit as Irish as the Citizen or any other Dubliner in *Ulysses*. That is, he lives in the United Kingdom, has the right to vote for a Member of Parliament, is subject to British law, and would carry a British passport if he travelled abroad.'[2] Although Joyce's novel alludes to this condition both explicitly and obliquely throughout its representation of Dublin, the political ramifications of its time and place came to the critical forefront in Joyce studies only relatively recently. In spite of roots in 1950s and 1960s Continental and African writing, the field of postcolonial theory and criticism made its major impact in literary studies much later, after the publication of Edward Said's 1978 *Orientalism*.[3] Enda Duffy's exploration of Irish nationalism in *Ulysses* – *The Subaltern 'Ulysses'* – was published in 1994 and preceded many of the other important postcolonial studies of Joyce's work that have since appeared.[4]

Rather than faulting the film for not anticipating the recent critical rediscoveries of Joycean nationalist literary politics, we might assess its politics against the critical trends of its filmmaking time, the 1960s. Jeffrey Segall reminds us that, paradoxically, it was the American New Critics of the 1950s and 60s who, with their apolitical and formalist bent, conferred 'full literary citizenship' on the modernist poets and novelists.[5] He writes: 'The effect of New Criticism was to decontextualize literature, to isolate it outside the social fabric and ignore its political import.'[6] Joseph Strick therefore ironically found a newly respectable, but depoliticized, Joyce to film, although it is telling that the Joyce critic he claims to have heeded most was the 'independent Marxist' Edmund Wilson, who made his mark in an earlier period, the 1930s.[7] Jeffrey Segall describes Wilson's construction of Joyce as a 'skilled but not heartless technician; as a fastidious recorder of the details of urban life and a prober of the secrets of the unconscious mind; and most importantly, as a liberal who advanced progressive human values'.[8] Joseph Strick's decision in the 1960s to foreground anti-Semitism, with its magnified post-World War II resonances, as the dominant political theme of his film of *Ulysses* can consequently be read as a progressive manoeuvre in face of the literary and critical ethos of his time. The film was made in an Ireland just prior to the new convulsions that racked Northern Ireland in 1969 after a failed civil rights campaign. Irish politics were not at the forefront for the film's projected Anglophone audience – particularly Americans – in 1966. Irish audiences would, no doubt, have been highly attentive to the film's representation of Irish political history, but due to Irish censorship the film was never shown there until the twenty-first century. Ironically, then, the film's shift to modernize the work's time and politics may have abetted its popularity at the time of its release – albeit at the price of the novel's political focus on Irish history. In the 1960s, anti-Semitism still reverberated as a global problem that could fruitfully replace British imperialism as a universal figure of oppression.

Nevertheless, a period film set in turn-of-the-century Ireland could have glossed more effectively the dense texture of allusion and incident that continually gestures towards Irish colonial history, and its history of resistance, in the novel. This is particularly true of the first episode, whose setting in the Martello tower invokes its ironic significance as a fortification built by William Pitt – not to protect Ireland but to thwart a possible Napoleonic strategy for using the country as an indirect approach to England. The point – merely oblique in the novel – does not translate to film and would have had even less relevance in the 1960s than in its Edwardian setting. More seriously, the film's later date mutes the potential for political conflict that lies just below the surface of the polite exchanges between the Oxford chap Haines and Stephen Dedalus. At the same time, it points to the problem of translating some of the chapter's political nuances cinematically. Joyce offers us a brilliant scene in the novel where the British Haines, as part of his Irish field research to collect Celtic folklore, speaks Gaelic to the uncomprehending old Irish milk-woman. 'Is it French you are talking, sir? the old woman said to Haines' (*Ulysses*, p. 12). The difficulty is that the Gaelic words Haines speaks are never produced in the text – presumably because no one but Haines understands them. Enda Duffy writes of this scene: 'It is inevitable that readers would read this exchange as a bitterly ironic comment on the way in which the Irish have had their language taken from them by the colonizing power, to the point where they cannot even recognize it. Virtually all critics have found the fact that in an Irish novel the only character who speaks Irish is an Englishman highly ironic.'[9] But not even Duffy comments on the deeper implication of the elision: namely that not even the scene's narrator can understand the Gaelic. Had Joseph Strick filmed this scene, he would have had to invent the Gaelic that Haines speaks, and this would have violated the whole point of Joyce's making it silent, and thereby incomprehensible, to the reader of the text. The scene simply cannot be filmed the way it is written, and Joseph Strick therefore omits it.

Numerous other references and discussions of Irish history are omitted by the logic of the later periodization of the film. Several episodes in the novel are structured substantially around Irish political or politically inflected cultural issues – notably 'Aeolus', 'Cyclops' and 'Scylla and Charybdis'. The discussion of Irish oratory in the newspaper room, for example, refers to numerous Irish journalists, barristers and politicians familiar at the turn-of-the century but thoroughly arcane after the mid-century. The visually impressive moment when the Viceregal cavalcade carrying the British lord lieutenant of Ireland, the Earl of Dudley, and his wife, Lady Dudley, through the streets of Dublin on their way to their inauguration of the Mirus Bazaar would also be anachronistic in the film. The 'gratefully oppressed', as Joyce in his story 'After the Race' called enthusiastic Irish crowds at parades of foreign dignitaries, were no longer oppressed in 1966. But the cavalcade is also significant in the novel as the contemporary reminder of the traumatic moment of Irish history that occurred twenty-two years before its setting: the Phoenix Park murders of 6 May 1882. On that day the Invincibles, a splinter group of the Fenians, assassinated Lord Frederick Cavendish, the new British chief secretary of Ireland, and the Irish under-secretary in Dublin Castle, Thomas Burke. The event occurred in Phoenix Park, not far from the Viceregal Lodge, and is discussed at various moments in the novel. Miles Crawford, the editor of the *Evening Telegraph*, talks about it, as do the men in Barney Kiernan's pub in 'Cyclops'. And Bloom repeats the rumour that the cabman's shelter, to which he takes Stephen Dedalus on their way to his home from the brothel, is run by one of the Invincibles named Skin-the-Goat. James Fairhall claims that 'The Phoenix Park murders lie at the center of *Ulysses*, at least insofar as Joyce uses the novel as a vehicle for a meditation on the nature of history, and of Irish history in particular.'[10] But their relevance as a subject of narrative, myth, rumour, and political fervour was already fading in 1904, according to Fairhall, and would have made little sense as a lively subject of popular discussion in the 1960s, when political attention had shifted to the North of Ireland.

But if an updated *Ulysses* creates a more international and universalized interpretation of the novel, it would have been none the less disastrous had the film lost the centrality that Ireland and Dublin hold in its imagined world. Joyce impressed on the young Arthur Power the importance of writing as an Irishman even if one had international ambitions – 'you are an Irishman and you must write in your own tradition', he is said to have told him. He went on to say: 'For myself, I always write about Dublin, because if I can get to the heart of Dublin I can get to the heart of all the cities in the world. In the particular is contained the universal.'[11] Joseph Strick honoured the significance of *Ulysses* as an Irish metropolitan epic by filming it almost entirely in Dublin, and by populating its scenes with a huge Irish cast. In the film, Dublin is given a sprawling and complex geography of varied horizontal and vertical topographies of seascapes, landscapes and a variety of urban streets, bridges, monuments and buildings fronting all sorts of public and private interiors. Richard Kain commends the film on its careful selection of locales that allow it to convey 'the same effect as the book, an atmosphere of teeming life in a shabby environment. We have the Blooms' cheap floral wallpaper and jangling brass bed.'[12] Strick's film does not evade Dublin's relative poverty, as when it points to the pawnshop to which Simon Dedalus carries his intellectual son's books.[13] The film also foregrounds the city's aesthetic dimension, although Strick carefully eschews postcard-pretty shots.[14] His black-and-white photography is evocative of old photographs of turn-of-the century Dublin without falsifying its modernity. A similar logic was evoked more recently when Steven Spielberg's cinematographer, Janusz Kaminski, decided to film *Schindler's List* (1993) in the black-and-white palette that recalled to him Roman Vishniak's earlier photographs of Jewish settlements collected in *A Vanished World* (1947). 'The imaginative camerawork,' Clifford Terry writes, 'effectively captures the misty bleakness of Dublin'.[15]

Nor is Strick's cinematic representation of the city and its people without ideological significance. Enda Duffy writes in his book: '*Ulysses*, for reasons to do with the politics of its critical reception, has almost without exception been read as a text that ultimately despised the city, the people, and the would-be nation in which, paradoxically, it shows an obsessive interest.'[16] As an interpretation of the novel, Joseph Strick's *Ulysses* dramatically reverses this attitude. The film quite embraces Dublin and its people with a generous affection, and even accepts its betrayers, usurpers and bigots as necessary evils for its realism. Some of this charismatic evocation of Dublin may have been an effect of Strick's experience in filming his *Ulysses* almost entirely in the city, including the interior scenes, which presumably could have been shot in a studio elsewhere rather than on location.[17] Produced by a British company in the 1960s, the Strick film qualified for a special subsidy administered by the British Film Fund called the 'Eady' subsidy, named after the parliamentarian who promoted its legislation. The subsidy, which taxed revenues from foreign (chiefly US) films and returned them to British filmmakers stipulated the use of British union crews,[18] which in turn included Irish members whose familiarity with the city was a great help in filming *Ulysses*. Joseph Strick found that getting permission to film all around Dublin and inside its public buildings was entirely unproblematic. The city and its people were endlessly obliging, going so far as to stop the main-line trains during the filming of the night sequences in order not to ruin the film's soundtrack. The sense we get as readers of *Ulysses*, that the Dublin of 1904 is a lively modern city with the ethos of a homely village, seems to have perdured into the sixties when Strick set up shop to film there. Stephen Watts's 1966 *New York Times* article described the production company set-up in Dublin during the shooting of the film. Two adjacent modern houses on a quiet suburban street in Ballsbridge served as headquarters – one as the production office and the other as Strick's residence and office where two secretaries assisted him with the work. Watts notes that the 'hideous' cuckoo clock that identifies Bloom as a 'cuckold' in the film was mounted on the wall of Strick's Ballsbridge living room. The interiors of both the Blooms' 7 Eccles Street residence and Bella Cohen's brothel were actually filmed in a large house in Sandymount that served as a studio for interiors.[19] However, Strick tried as much as possible to use the actual locales mentioned in the novel for the outdoor settings. He filmed the opening sequence at the Martello Tower and the Forty Foot swimming cove in Sandymount. 7 Eccles Street was still standing in 1966, and when Bloom, having forgotten his key, drops into the front entry well to get into his house through the kitchen, it is 7 Eccles street he is shown entering.

The city of Dublin itself becomes a character in the film, made even more vivid in its visual than its novelistic representation as a city of infinite variety. The film offers scenes of O'Connell Street, the Ha'penny Bridge, the colonnade of the Bank of Ireland, St George's Church, their aesthetic function none the less subordinated to their roles as *mise-en-scène* for the peripatetic citizenry. Bosley Crowther enjoys the city's modernity in the film: 'The streets are full of automobiles. The quays along the river are crowded with modern ships.'[20] The Dublin waterways are enlivened with the sights and sounds of birds as we see flocks of gulls over Sandymount Strand and over the Liffey. The camera observes them, as does Bloom – 'Looking down he saw flapping strongly, wheeling between the gaunt quaywalls, gulls' (*Ulysses*, p. 125). The film's black-and-white palette captures the glinting of light that plays over the water surfaces, a lighting that becomes even more dramatic at night in the stunning overhead shot of the gleaming river with its twinkling bridges and Dublin's multitudinous city lights. Paddy Dignam's funeral was shot at Glasnevin cemetery, whose Celtic crosses, tombstones and statuary transform the burial ground into a literal petrified forest. The film's funeral procession with its horse-drawn cortège was not an anachronism. Strick was able to hire horses and carriages from a commercial funeral establishment because the kind of ornate hearse bearing Paddy Dignam's coffin to Glasnevin was still used for funerals in 1966. On the way to the funeral the carriage bearing Bloom, Dedalus, Cunningham and Power is stopped beside the Grand Canal, where they see the gasworks in the novel. Strick uses the moment to show industrial Dublin with its smokestacks, counterparts to the church spires elsewhere in the film.

If the visual images of Dublin – from its Georgian landmarks to its pawnshops and outdoor bookstalls in narrow lanes – evoke the city, so do its sounds, the speech of its denizens, its music and its assorted clamour. The 'Irishness' of Joseph Strick's *Ulysses* is in the end even more auditory than visual, with Irish speech itself a star of the film. Archer Winsten's review in the *New York Post* commends the film for just this aspect of its translation:

> One thinks of the countless movies that have attempted one way or another to turn the charm of Ireland to entertainment. Those were full of falsity, professional Irish, stage Irish, joke Irish, colour Irish. But here are the real Irish, Joyce's own, presented with bitterness, and truth, and human frailty, and with that grandiloquent eloquence and blasphemy that Joyce alone could quarry out of the old sod and the people thereof.[21]

Although two of the leading actors in the film were not Irish, Joseph Strick was mindful of giving his scenes the sound of English spoken by assorted Irish tongues. British Barbara Jefford's Molly Bloom easily produces the Irish idioms and Dublin locutions Joyce gives her soliloquy, spoken in a lilting, lyrical performance. Strick recalls that he filmed Molly's monologue first: 'Once we had it, I knew we had a movie'. Written English is difficult to produce with its Irish inflection made audible – as we see in the conscious deformations Joyce had to introduce into the 'Anna Livia Plurabelle' section of *Finnegans Wake* to give his washerwomen a genuine-sounding vernacular. The washerwomen themselves draw attention to Irish speech: 'And his derry's own drawl and his corksown blather and his doubling stutter and his gullaway swank.'[22] Strick provides an interesting justification for Barbara Jefford's arguably 'mixed' accent by reminding us that Molly Bloom was raised in Gibraltar, a British garrison town that might have given her an accent more 'doubling' – as Joyce might put it – than Dublin.[23] Martin Dempsey was cast as Simon Dedalus as much for his Cork accent ('corksown blather') as for his marvellous voice performing 'Love's Old Sweet Song'. The film's script carefully preserves precisely those conversations and scenes in the novel that highlight the *art* of the Irish raconteur: the wit of Simon Dedalus's locutions ('I'll tickle his catastrophe'), the cemetery joke told in Glasnevin ('Not a bloody bit like the man'), the indignant emphasis of the accused Mary Driscoll ('As God is looking down on me this day if ever I laid a hand to them oylsters!'). If the star of Joyce's novel is the vigour not only of the literary prose but also of the robust vernacular of Irish idiom ('It's as uncertain as a child's bottom'), so the star of Strick's *Ulysses* is the collective performance of its ensemble of largely Irish actors.

'I was amazed at the richness and variety, discipline, professionalism and sheer talent available in Dublin', Joseph Strick says of his casting of the film. He recalls that there were three major theatrical enterprises in the city at that time: the Abbey Theatre, the Gate Theatre and the Radio Telefís Éireann Players. 'I was able to cast 60 speaking parts with wonderful choices without inconveniencing the theatre companies.'[24] Many of the actors, like Barbara Jefford, had extensive stage experience but little film experience, though they adapted quickly to the new medium and, indeed, a number of them enjoyed highly successful film and television careers thereafter. Fionnula Flanagan, the Abbey Theatre-trained actress, had her first film role, as Gerty MacDowell, in Strick's *Ulysses* before she went on to play multiple characters in the film *James Joyce's Women* (dir. Michael Pearse, 1985). She later played Annie Higgins in *Some Mother's Son* (dir. Terry George, 1996), as well as Annie O'Shea in *Waking Ned Divine* (dir. Kirk Jones, 1998), and appeared in numerous television shows including the series *Rich Man, Poor Man*, *Columbo* and, most recently, a 2003 film version of *Murder She Wrote*. Milo O'Shea's career later encompassed a variety of roles in films as diverse as Zefferelli's *Romeo and Juliet* (1968), *Barbarella* (dir. Roger Vadim, 1968), *The Verdict* (dir. Sidney Lumet, 1982) and *The Butcher Boy* (dir. Neil Jordan, 1997). T. P. McKenna, Martin Dempsey, Anna Manahan and many of the others have since enjoyed regular roles in films, television series and stage performances, but their breakthrough came with *Ulysses*. Strick encouraged the actors to contribute to the shaping of their roles. He explains: 'It is my method (as it is with some other directors) to avoid giving direction until there is a first look at what the actor has in mind, since if the performer is told what to do, most will do so without trying out their own ideas.'[25] Viewing the film, the inventiveness of the Dublin actors is everywhere apparent, but particularly in the most challenging sequence of the film, the 'Nighttown' scenes of 'Circe'. The comedic training and experience of a number of the actors in the music halls contributed distinctly to the vaudeville character of this episode. Critic Cheryl Herr has traced the theatrical roots of 'Circe' to the Victorian Pantomime,[26] while other critics point to its kinship with Continental Expressionist drama, but Joseph Strick's interpretation gave it much of the character of an olio, or a miscellany of skits and turns on the comedy stage. Milo O'Shea and Maureen Potter, who played Josie Breen, were highly successful music-hall comedians when they were recruited for the film, and their verbal duet, 'You were the lion of the night with your seriocomic recitation . . . Ladies and gentlemen, I give you Ireland, home and beauty', remains one of the most charming bits of business in the 'Nighttown' sequence.

Plate 16. Bloom imitating the statue.

The film also effectively theatricalizes Dublin's urban spaces during the 'Nighttown' sequence with the effect of ironizing Irish politics – or at least Bloom's fantasies of them. Bloom's extravagant fantasy ambitions, ranging from socialist reformer to emperor, are set off by outdoor venues replete with statuary and monuments as well as by spacious indoor venues that gesture towards the city's history. Strick credits Milo O'Shea, who posed like a statue (Plate 16) when delivering such lines as 'You have the advantage of me. Lady Bloom accepts no presents', for suggesting the use of public statuary as an ironic analogue for Bloom's political posturings in 'Circe'. Insofar as statuary monuments freeze statesmen and notable citizens in histrionic and heroic poses, they provide visual models for fantasies of political and public success. When these monuments were erected in honour of British military or naval heroes, their role in the Dublin capital intensifies their irony. Joyce lampooned one of the most notorious of these – the statue of Admiral Nelson atop Nelson's Pillar on O'Connell Street – by having Stephen Dedalus call the British hero a 'onehandled adulterer' (*Ulysses*, p. 121). Nelson's Pillar was damaged by an explosion in March 1966, the fiftieth anniversary of the 1916 Easter uprising, and torn down just before the filming of *Ulysses* began. Stephen's little story of the two Dublin spinsters and their excursion to the top of the Pillar is elided from the film at little cost, since neither Admiral Nelson's amputation nor his scandalous affair with Lady Emma Hamilton would have held much significance for 1960s viewers. However, Bloom in 'Nighttown' declaims in the shadow of the Wellington monument, which was dedicated to the

Plate 17. The coronation of Bloom.

Plate 18. Bloom and Stephen in the kitchen.

Dublin-born militarist who defeated Napoleon at Waterloo and later served as a British prime minister. Bloom also strikes 'poses as municipal reformer . . . identical to those of Grattan and other figures on Dublin monuments'.[27] Even Molly Bloom is not spared statuesque parody and, when she grieves a bit too sentimentally over the death of Rudy, the film poses her with some maudlin funerary statuary. The film also uses monumental indoor spaces ironically for Bloom's political 'Nighttown' fantasies. The venue of Bloom's kangaroo trial is set in the venerable trial hall of the Four Courts, whose historical role in the administration of British justice in Ireland was repaid by bombardment during the Civil War in 1922. The vision of Bloom's coronation as King of Ireland (Plate 17) creates an ironic contrast with the populist John Stuart Parnell's epithet as Ireland's 'uncrowned king'. (The scene quotes the oath the English sovereign takes at his coronation, but substitutes 'Ireland' for 'England'.) And the coronation's setting in the magnificent halls of Dublin Castle – 'the seat of English rule in Ireland until it was taken over by the provisional government in 1922'[28] – makes Bloom's royalist fantasies particularly politically ironic.

The most beautiful and significant visual setting in the film is, of course, Howth Head, the site of Molly and Bloom's first lovemaking and the marriage proposal acceptance, recalled by both in memory. The novel brilliantly captures the deep emotional significance this site has for both husband and wife, but it cannot convey its dramatic visual beauty. Even in black and white, the film can instantly dramatize what Bennett's *Encyclopaedia of Dublin* describes: 'Howth Head is one of the most striking features of north Dublin's coastline. Its rounded contours rising from the sea and the low outline of the isthmus give it the appearance of an island.'[29] The film not only conveys this sense of Howth as looking and feeling like an island, but

Plate 19. Molly in bed.

Plate 20. Molly and Bloom on Howth Head.

it dilates the emotional significance of this sensation in important ways. By juxtaposing scenes of Howth with scenes actually filmed in Gibraltar[30] the film visually establishes the startling topographical congruence between the two vistas. This in turn reinforces the logic of Molly's imaginative and emotional oscillation between these two romantic locales of different moments of her past. With its evocations of Mediterranean lushness and cultural complexity, including lovely shots of the Barbary apes at the height of the Rock, Molly's sensuality is given a kind of natural origin in the film. At the same time, the film suggests visually how the elevated vista of Howth conspires to create an aura of transcendence, the feeling of this elevated place as rising above the quotidian life below and as somehow nearer to heaven. Following on from Molly's long reverie of a day full of sexual and romantic images alternating with homely images of the ordinary – little girls skipping with rope, fish being gutted, ladies' drawers on a line with a burn mark from the iron – the memories of Howth and Gibraltar move Molly's thoughts and sensations to another plane in the film. The soliloquy makes clear that nature inspires Molly with something like religious fervour: 'God of heaven theres nothing like nature the wild mountains then the sea and the waves rushing then the beautiful country.' Near the end of the soliloquy the film, in uncharacteristically bald symbolism, interpolates images of stained-glass windows and church interiors – man-made vistas designed also to stimulate awe – into Molly's reveries of natural beauty and evocations of emotional intensity. The effect works successfully to counterbalance the unvarnished sexual candour of her prose by conveying the implied suggestion that sexuality is for Molly at times closer to the sacred than to the profane. At the same time, the film's evocation of Howth as an island lends the scenes there an aura of emotional privacy and emotional privilege. The Blooms as young lovers on a holiday running along the ridge of the hill appear free of all earthly cares (Plate 20), and free to give themselves over to pure beauty and pure pleasure. We may not see the rhododendrons Molly remembers so vividly in memory, but we do see the grasses stirring in the wind in the film. And their mild agitation serves as a subtle analogue for the agitation of their bodies ('and his heart was going like mad') as the lovers both make love and love.

CREDITS

Title	Ulysses
Director	Joseph Strick
Release Year	1967
Production Company	Ulysses Film Production
Country	Great Britain

Cast:

Milo O'Shea	Leopold Bloom
Barbara Jefford	Molly Bloom
Maurice Roëves	Stephen Dedalus
T.P. McKenna	Buck Mulligan
Anna Manahan	Bella Cohen
Maureen Potter	Josie Breen
Martin Dempsey	Simon Dedalus
Graham Lines	Haines
Joe Lynch	Blazes Boylan
Fionnula Flanagan	Gerty MacDowell
Maire Hastings	Mary Driscoll
Geoffrey Golden	The Citizen
Dave Kelly	Garrett Deasy
Maureen Toal	Zoe Higgins
Rosaleen Linehan	Nurse Callan
Sheila O'Sullivan	May Goulding Dedalus
O.Z. Whitehead	Alexander J. Dowie
Leon Collins	Lynch
Des Perry	Bantam Lyons
Tony Doyle	Lt. Gardner
Claire Mullen	Florry
Pamela Mant	Kitty
Peter Maycock	Jack Power
Chris Curran	Myles Crawford
Biddie White-Lennon	Cissy Caffrey
Eddie Golden	Martin Cunningham
Meryl Gourley	The Hon. Mrs. Mervyn Talboys
Robert Carlisle Jr.	Dr. Dixon
Ann Rowan	Mrs. Bellingham
Des Keogh	Joe Hynes
Robert Somerset	Lenehan

Cecil Sheridan	John Henry Manton
May Cluskey	Mrs. Yelverton Barry
John Molloy	Corny Kelleher
Ruadhan Neeson	Cyril Sargent
James Bartley	Pte. Carr
Colin Bird	Pte. Compton
Jack Plant	Denis Breen
Paddy Roche	Madden
Eugene Lambert	Costello
Danny Cummins	The Drinker
Brendan Cauldwell	Bob Doran

Credits:

Joseph Strick	Director
Walter Reade Jr.	Executive Producer
Joseph Strick	Producer
Wilfrid Eades	Associate Producer
Fred Haines	Associate Producer
Pat Green	Production Manager
Betty Batley	Production Assistant
Kevin Fitzsimons	Location liaison
Dennis Robertson	Assistant Director
Joseph Strick	Script
Fred Haines	Script
James Joyce	Original novel
Wolfgang Suschitzky	Photography
Séamus Corcoran	Camera Operator
Reginald Mills	Editor
Graham Probst	Art Director
Betty Long	Wardrobe
Stanley Myers	Music composed and conducted
Christian Wangler	Sound

Running Time	132
Field Length	11903 ft or 3630 mtrs.
Colour Code	Black/White
Sound System	Panavision

Notes to Chapter 1

1.   Andrée D. Sheehy Skeffington reproduced this play from a typed copy found in Hanna Sheehy Skeffington's papers in the Spring 1984 issue of the *James Joyce Quarterly*, pp. 205–215. She also discusses the context of Joyce's performance.

2.   Peter Costello, *James Joyce: the Years of Growth 1882–1915* (New York: Pantheon, 1993), p. 159.

3.   Richard Ellmann, *James Joyce*. (New York: Oxford University Press, rev. ed. 1982), p. 70.

4.   *The Critical Writings of James Joyce*, eds. Ellsworth Mason and Richard Ellmann (Ithaca: Cornell University Press, 1989), p. 44.

5.   *Critical Writings*, p. 45.

6.   Ellmann, p. 74.

7.   Ellmann, p. 75.

8.   Ellmann, p. 79.

9.   *Critical Writings*, p. 70.

10.   James Joyce, *Dubliners* (New York: Penguin Books, 1996), p. 49.

11.   Stanislaus Joyce, *My Brother's Keeper* (New York: Viking Press, 1958), p. 90.

12.   Alan Spiegel, *Fiction and the Camera Eye* (Charlottesville: University Press of Virginia, 1976), p. 77.

13.   Ellmann, p. 300.

14.   A highly detailed and informative account of Joyce's involvement with the Volta movie enterprise was published in *Nordic Rejoycings 1982: In Commemoration of the Centenary of the Birth of James Joyce* (Norberg: Uno Johansons Tryckeri AB, 1982) pp. 125–136, by Gösta Werner. Philip Sicker's forthcoming essay, 'Evenings at the Volta: Cinematic Afterimages in Joyce', further makes a persuasive argument that Joyce was keenly interested in the aesthetic and social ramifications of the new medium and its potentially enriching effects on Irish audiences. See also Costello, pp. 290–293, for another comprehensive account of the Volta enterprise.

15.   Ellmann, p. 210.

16.   Ellmann, p. 510.

17.   Ellmann, pp. 426–457.

18.   These two letters are reprinted in two different volumes. See letter to Harriet Shaw Weaver, 27 June 1924, in *Letters of James Joyce*, ed. Stuart Gilbert (New York: The Viking Press, 1957), p. 216. Also letter to Harriet Shaw, 23 December 1924, in *Letters of James Joyce*, Vol. III, ed. Richard Ellmann (New York: The Viking Press, 1966), p. 112.

19. Ellmann, p. 561.
20. Werner, p. 494.
21. Werner, p. 497.
22. *Beyond the Stars: the Memoirs of Sergei Eisenstein*, ed. Richard Taylor, trans. William Powell (Calcutta: Seagull Books, 1995), p. 368.
23. Werner, p. 496.
24. Ellmann, p. 654.
25. This passage, and the description of the illegible dedication, are cited in Werner, p. 496.
26. *Beyond the Stars*, pp. 5, 216.
27. Werner, p. 498.
28. Emily Tall, 'Eisenstein on Joyce: Sergei Eisenstein's Lecture on James Joyce at the State Institute of Cinematography, November 1, 1934', *James Joyce Quarterly*, Vol. 24, No. 2 (Winter 1987), pp. 133–142.
29. Jeffrey Segall, *Joyce in America: Cultural Politics and the Trials of 'Ulysses'* (Berkeley: University of California Press, 1993), p. 27.
30. Tall, pp. 134, 137.
31. Letter from Paul Léon to Ralph Pinker, 26 October 1932, in *Letters of James Joyce*, Vol. III, pp. 262–263.
32. Thomas L. Burkdall, *Joycean Frames: Film and the Fiction of James Joyce* (New York: Routledge, 2001), p. 17.
33. Letter to George Joyce, 29 October 1934, in *Letters of James Joyce*, Vol. III, pp. 326–327.
34. *Letters of James Joyce*, Vol. III, p. 380.
35. Burkdall, pp. 5, xiv.
36. Both Lucie Noël's story and Mary Colum's are cited by Burkdall, p. 6.
37. William York Tindall, *A Reader's Guide to 'Finnegans Wake'* (New York: Farrar, 1969).
38. Costello, p. 292.

Notes to Chapter 2

1. Stephen Watts, 'Movies: "If you Censor 'Ulysses' There Will be a Scandal"', *New York Times* (Sunday 2 October 1966), p. D11.
2. Joseph Strick, e-mail to Margot Norris, 13 March 2003.
3. Joseph Strick, e-mail to Margot Norris, 2 March 2003.
4. Michael Dwyer, 'Strick, Bearing Bawdy Greeks, Sees "Ulysses" Come Home at Last,' *Irish Times* (11 November 2000), p. W6.
5. Joseph Strick, e-mail to Margot Norris, 7 March 2003.

6.   Joseph Strick, e-mail to Margot Norris, 2 March 2003.

7.   Joseph Strick, e-mail to Margot Norris, 7 March 2003.

8.   Joseph Strick, e-mail to Margot Norris, 4 March 2003.

9.   Joseph Strick, e-mail to Margot Norris, 3 March 2003.

10.   Watts, p. D11

11.   Joseph Strick, e-mail to Margot Norris, 2 March 2003. There seems to have been some confusion about the film's budget, possibly in relation to whether distribution costs were factored in, in Stephen Watts' 1966 *New York Times* piece. Watts reports that Walter Reade, Jr, 'undertook half the financing – about $500,000 – and, for the rest, put the proposition to British Lion, of which he is a director' (2 October 1966, p. D11). Edward Murray, who seems to rely on the 1966 Watts interview with Strick for much of his information, reports that 'The completed film was produced for about a million dollars, a mere pittance by Hollywood standards'. *The Cinematic Imagination* (New York: Frederick Ungar Publishing, 1972), p. 131.

12.   Joseph Strick, e-mail to Margot Norris, 13 March 2003.

13.   'Maurice Roëves: A Heart-to-Heart with Col. Munro', interview with Mohican Press, October 1998, <www.mohicanpress.com/m006012.html>.

14.   Watts, p. D11.

15.   Since this claim was made before filming was complete, it may be a bit hyperbolic.

16.   See Kevin Barry's discussion of the divergences from Joyce's text in the Huston film of 'The Dead', *The Dead* (Cork: Cork University Press, 2001), p. 47.

17.   Paul Cullen, 'Director Threatens Legal Action over New *Ulysses* Film', *Irish Times* (19 June 2001), p. 25.

18.   Pauline Kael, *Kiss Kiss Bang Bang* (New York: Atlantic Monthly Press Book, 1968), p. 170.

19.   Matthew Hodgart and Mabel P. Worthington, *Songs in the Work of James Joyce* (New York: Columbia University Press, 1959).

20.   Bosley Crowther, review of Joseph Strick's *Ulysses*, *New York Times* (13 March 1967), p. 55:1.

21.   Joseph Strick, e-mail to Margot Norris, 7 March 2003.

22.   Joseph Strick, e-mail to Margot Norris, 4 March 2003.

23.   Watts, p. D11.

24.   Joseph Strick, e-mail to Margot Norris, 3 March 2003.

25.   Joseph Strick, e-mail to Margot Norris, 3 March 2003.

26.   Joseph Strick, e-mail to Margot Norris, 4 March 2003.

27.   Joseph Strick, e-mail to Margot Norris, 4 March 2003.

Notes to Chapter 3

1. <www.randomhouse.com/modern library/100best/novels>.
2. Thom Bennett, 'A Conversation with Maverick Filmmaker Joseph Strick' (31 March 2001) <www.filmthreat.com/interviews>.
3. T. S. Eliot, ' "Ulysses", Order, and Myth', *Selected Prose of T. S. Eliot*, ed. Frank Kermode (New York: Farrar, Straus and Giroux, 1975), pp. 175–178.
4. Karen Lawrence, *The Odyssey of Style in 'Ulysses'* (Princeton: Princeton University Press, 1981).
5. James Joyce, *A Portrait of the Artist as a Young Man*, ed. Chester G. Anderson (New York: Viking Press, 1968), p. 203.
6. Hugh Kenner published an early essay in which he points out that Joyce, who had no professional knowledge of Greek, would have encountered Homer's work in translation, and therefore would have encountered many Homers. He thinks it particularly likely that Joyce may have been familiar with a translation of the *Odyssey* by Samuel Henry Butcher and Andrew Lang, and another by Samuel Butler. In his view, these Homers would have provided Joyce with a particularly novelistic or 'realistic' version of the *Odyssey*. See Hugh Kenner, 'Homer's Sticks and Stones', *James Joyce Quarterly*, Vol. 6, No. 4 (Summer 1969), pp. 285–298.
7. James Joyce, *Ulysses*, ed. Hans Walter Gabler with Wolfhard Steppe and Claus Melchior (New York: Random House, Inc., 1986). All subsequent references will be cited in the text.
8. T. E. Hulme, *Speculations: Essays on Humanism and the Philosophy of Art* (London: Routledge and Kegan Paul, 1958), pp. 111–140.
9. Eliot, p. 175.
10. Eliot, p. 177.
11. Joyce, *Portrait*, p. 205.
12. Richard Ellmann's review of the film in *The New York Review of Books* treats the omission of Stephen's lecture and the discussions of the pressmen in the newsroom as a censorship of the intellect. He writes, 'But with all its small boldnesses, the film displays a new kind of bowdlerizing. Instead of expurgating the body, it expurgates the mind. Masturbation is in, cogitation is out. The discussion of *Hamlet* in the library is censored away, as is the discussion of rhetoric in the newspaper episode.' See 'Bloomovie', *The New York Review of Books* (15 June 1967), pp. 12–13.
13. Harry Blamires, *The New Bloomsday Book: a Guide through 'Ulysses'*, third edition (New York: Routledge, 1996), p. 199.
14. Lawrence, p. 167.

15. See Mary Power, 'The Discovery of *Ruby*', *James Joyce Quarterly*, Vol. 18, No. 2 (Winter 1981), pp. 115–122.
16. Lawrence, pp. 4–5.
17. Lawrence, pp. 10–11.

Notes to Chapter 4

1. Watts, p. D11. William Glackin's review of the film in *The Sacramento Bee* suggests that it worked well for both audiences: 'I would also guess – and was told last night by a reliable witness – that you do not have to have read the book to enjoy [the film].' See William C. Glackin, '"Ulysses" Comes Out a Superb Movie', *The Sacramento Bee* (15 March 1967), p. B10.
2. Ellmann, 'Bloomovie', p. 13.
3. Judith Crist, 'A Superb Screen Translation of Joyce's "Ulysses"', *New York Herald Tribune–Washington Post* (16 March 1967), p. 5.
4. Arthur Power, *Conversations with Joyce*, ed. Clive Hart (Chicago: University of Chicago Press, 1982), pp. 73–74.
5. Some critics, however, found themselves extremely moved by Roëves's performance. 'For Daedalus [*sic*], Strick selected a gaunt, young actor with pensive, deep-set eyes, and hollow cheeks. Maurice Roëves has simply to look into the camera and the vision in his eyes seems to circumvent the world, returning from some starry height to penetrate inward', wrote the reviewer in the *Berkeley Daily Gazette* (17 March 1967), p. 10. Charles Champlin even describes him as 'looking slightly like a mature Paul McCartney' – a comparison that made better sense in 1967 than it does now. See Charles Champlin, 'Joyce's "Ulysses" Makes Film Transition', *Los Angeles Times* (10 May 1967), IV, pp. 1, 16.
6. Susan Bazargan suggests an alternative possibility, that the 'headings' in the 'Aeolus' episode of the novel can actually be thought of as silent movie subtitles. See 'The Headings in "Aeolus": a Cinematographic View', *James Joyce Quarterly*, Vol. 23, No. 3 (Spring 1986), p. 345.
7. The canine representation may owe more to the pragmatic exigencies of filmmaking than to political symbolism, however. When I asked Joseph Strick why he transformed Garryowen from a mongrel to an Alsatian, he explained that scenes such as Garryowen's attack require pre-trained animals, which are generally available only as pedigreed breeds.

8.   Joyce, *Ulysses*, p. 283.
9.   Since Boylan is a figure in the novel who appears throughout chiefly in the perception of others, establishing his identity is difficult in the film. The posters conjoining his face and name, and the shop sign with his name, are film inventions designed to establish and underline Boylan's identity.
10.   Richard L. Coe, 'Joyce Evokes a Superb Film', *Washington Post* (15 March 1967), p. C11.
11.   Ellmann, 'Bloomovie', p. 12.
12.   Ray Loynd, '"Ulysses": Uncompromising as a Movie', *Los Angeles–Herald Examiner*, (10 May 1967), p. F2.
13.   Ellmann, 'Bloomovie', p. 12. Richard M. Kain, 'Ulysses on Film', *James Joyce Quarterly*, Vol. 4, No. 4 (Summer 1967), pp. 351–353.
14.   Richard Kain writes of the variety of Blooms portrayed by Milo O'Shea in these sequences: 'Bloom in court, Bloom in the circus ring, Bloom in the operating room, nude, with derby as fig-leaf, are memorable.' See Kain, p. 351.
15.   Crowther, p. 55:1.
16.   Richard Coe predicts that they 'would probably curl the hair' of the casual moviegoer (Coe, p. C11). Clifford Terry calls the language 'coarse' and although he concedes that they 'certainly haven't been inserted for shock value . . . their exclusion wouldn't have detracted from the overall mood' See Terry, 'Controversial "Ulysses" Film Excellent', *Chicago Tribune* (15 March 1967), Section 2, pp. 1–2. *Hollywood Reporter* (10 May 1967), p. 3, predicted that 'The language, employing all the four-letter words, will startle some.'
17.   But the staging of both Bloom's socialist and Zionist fantasies gains at least some provocative resonance from the film's setting in the post-McCarthy era of the Cold War, and in the decades after the establishment of Israel as a state in 1948. Likewise, Bloom's 'Nighttown' utopian wish to achieve the unification of 'jew, muslim, and gentile' appears even more poignant in the third year of the twenty-first century than in 1904, 1922 or 1966.
18.   Joseph Valente links the pub drinkers' own imperilled masculinity as colonial subjects to their gender aggressions against the Jewish Bloom: 'The shifting of Bloom's position from father to mother, the mockery of his uxoriousness and maternal solicitude, the skepticism as to his sexual experience, the citizen's pointed question, all of this extends the strategy . . . to transpose the double-bind of Irish manhood on to the received stereotype of Jewish femininity.' See Joseph Valente, '"Neither fish nor flesh"; or how "Cyclops" stages

the double-bind of Irish manhood', *Semicolonial Joyce*, eds. Derek Attridge and Marjorie Howes (Cambridge: Cambridge University Press, 2000), p. 123.

19. Ray Loynd, p. F2. However, Joseph Strick concedes that there is one moment in Molly Bloom's soliloquy that left him at a loss as to what visual image might be a plausible correlative: when she says 'whats the idea of making us like that with a big hole in the middle of us'. The dilemma reminded Strick of an old Jewish joke:

> So this guy sees a shop window full of clocks and asks to buy one of them. The shopkeeper says, 'We don't sell clocks.'
> The guy says, 'What do you do?'
> Shopkeeper: 'I'm a mull.' (A performer of circumcisions).
> Guy: 'Then why to you have a window full of clocks?'
> Shopkeeper: 'What would *you* put in the window?'

Strick put a store-window full of clocks on the screen to illustrate Molly's words. (Joseph Strick e-mail to Margot Norris, 17 March 2003).

20. Kain, p. 352.
21. Louis Cook, '"Ulysses" Is Among the Great Films, But Don't Expect a Kids' Tea Party', *Detroit Free Press* (15 March 1967) p. 7C.
22. Richard L. Coe, 'Joyce Evokes a Superb Film', *Washington Post* (15 March 1967), p. C11.
23. Clifford Terry, 'Controversial "Ulysses" Film Excellent', *Chicago Tribune* (15 March 1967), pp. 1–2, Section 2.
24. Crowther, p. 55:1.
25. Crist, p. 5.
26 Kathleen McCormick gives a dark description of the critical climate of the 1950s and '60s with respect to Molly Bloom's reception. She writes, 'since the postwar period was a time of strong antifeminist sentiment, expressions of rage and horror at Molly's overtly sexual nature were fueled and encouraged by the general ideology'. See Kathleen McCormick, 'Reproducing Molly Bloom: a Revisionary History of the Reception of "Penelope", 1922–1970', *Molly Blooms: a Polylogue on 'Penelope' and Cultural Studies*, ed. Richard Pearce (Madison: University of Wisconsin Press, 1994), p. 21.
27. Kain, p. 352.
28. Champlin, p. 1, 16; Part IV.
29. Kimberly J. Devlin, 'Pretending in "Penelope": Masquerade,

Mimicry, and Molly Bloom', *Molly Blooms: A Polylogue on 'Penelope' and Cultural Studies*, ed. Richard Pearce (Madison: University of Wisconsin Press, 1994), p. 88.

30. Glackin, p. B10.

31. Spiegel, p. 78; Murray, pp. 133–134. Craig Wallace Barrow praises a number of effects in the film, especially the momentary blackening of the screen in 'Proteus', but says little else besides; see Craig Wallace Barrow, *Montage in James Joyce's 'Ulysses'* (Potomac, MD: Studia Humanitas, 1980), p. 38. For general discussions on Joyce and film, see Morris Beja, *Film and Literature: An Introduction* (New York: Longman, Inc., 1979), Richard Pearce, *The Novel in Motion: an Approach to Modern Fiction* (Columbus: Ohio State University Press, 1983), and Burkdall.

32. Paul Van Caspel, *Bloomers on the Liffey: Eisegetical Readings of Joyce's 'Ulysses'* (Baltimore: Johns Hopkins University Press, 1986); Haigwood, p. 10. Haigwood seems to have been misled by Bloom's bogus identification of himself as a 'dental surgeon' in the 'Nighttown' fantasy sequence.

33. Cook, p. 7C; Champlin, p. 16; Robert Sullivan, 'Joyce's "Ulysses" is Outstanding as Movie', *Capital Times* (13 March 1967), Green section, p. 4.

Notes to Chapter 5

1. Postcolonial criticism complicates even the simple term 'colony' as properly describing the relationship of Ireland to Britain during the time of Joyce's novel. The introduction to *Semicolonial Joyce* raises just this question: 'in analyzing the centuries-long relationship between Ireland and Britain, is it appropriate and useful to call that relationship "colonial" in any or all periods of its history?' See Derek Attridge and Marjorie Howes, eds., *Semicolonial Joyce* (Cambridge: Cambridge University Press, 2000), p. 7.

2. James Fairhall, *James Joyce and the Question of History* (Cambridge: Cambridge University Press, 1993), p. 170.

3. Edward W. Said, *Orientalism* (New York: Vintage, 1978).

4. Enda Duffy, *The Subaltern 'Ulysses'* (Minneapolis: University of Minnesota Press, 1994). Two other more general postcolonial studies of Joyce's work are Vincent J. Cheng, *Joyce, Race, and Empire* (Cambridge: Cambridge University Press, 1995), and Emer Nolan, *James Joyce and Nationalism* (London: Routledge, 1995).

5. Segall, p. 50.

6.   Segall, p. 120.
7.   Joseph Strick, e-mail to Margot Norris, 2 March 2003.
8.   Segall, p. 175.
9.   Duffy, p. 50.
10. Fairhall, p. 26.
11. Quoted in Ellmann, *James Joyce*, p. 505.
12. Kain, p. 351.
13. The film also retains the touching scene that shows Dilly Dedalus's hunger for knowledge exceeding her physical hunger, when she spends the coins wheedled from her father for milk and a bun on a French primer.
14. Joyce himself writes a cautionary parable about postcards of Dublin into *Ulysses* in the little story J. J. O'Molloy tells in the newsroom of 'Aeolus' about Lady Dudley, the wife of Ireland's British viceroy: 'Lady Dudley was walking home through the park to see all the trees that were blown down by that cyclone last year and thought she'd buy a view of Dublin. And it turned out to be a commemoration postcard of Joe Brady or Number One or Skin-the-Goat. Right outside the viceregal lodge, imagine!' (Joyce, *Ulysses*, p. 113). People who want to see Dublin as a pretty picture, the anecdote implies, may and should be shocked by its scenes of natural and political devastation.
15. Terry, Section 2, p. 1.
16. Duffy, p. 2.
17. Kevin Barry discusses the pains John Huston's crew went through to recreate an authentically appointed Morkan House in a California suburb, since the filmmaker's failing health prohibited filming *The Dead* in Dublin (Barry, pp. 32–33).
18. Strick remembers that the stipulations entailed a fair amount of featherbedding. 'The union demanded that we have a crew size left over from the Middle Ages. Four sound technicians were required: we needed only two, for the technology had changed and the man whose duty was to watch the galvanometer on the sound film strip was made redundant by magnetic sound recording. We paid him to stay home and do his gardening in England and never met him.' (Joseph Strick, e-mail to Margot Norris, 9 May 2003.)
19. Watts, p. D11. Strick adds, 'When making films on location I've usually found a big derelict house in which to redecorate rooms for use when the weather prevented outdoor shooting. These are houses that even a film crew cannot damage!' (Joseph Strick, e-mail to Margot Norris, 16 July 2003.)

20. Crowther, p. 55:1.
21. Archer Winsten, '"Ulysses" Opens at 12 Theaters', *New York Post* (14 March 1967), p. 70.
22. James Joyce, *Finnegans Wake* (New York: Penguin Books, 1967), p. 197.
23. However, Molly herself suggests that she acquired an Irish accent from her father, in spite of growing up in Gibraltar. She thinks of her old British flame, Gardner: 'I was afraid he mightnt like my accent first he so English all father left me in spite of his stamps' (Joyce, *Ulysses*, p. 627).
24. (Joseph Strick, e-mail to Margot Norris, 10 May 2003.)
25. (Joseph Strick, e-mail to Margot Norris, 10 May 2003.)
26. Cheryl Herr, *Joyce's Anatomy of Culture* (Urbana: University of Illinois Press, 1986).
27. Kain, p. 351.
28. Douglas Bennett, *Encyclopaedia of Dublin* (Dublin: Gill & Macmillan, 1991), p. 59.
29. Bennett, p. 102
30. Kain finds the scenes of Gibraltar 'so similar to Howth that one wonders whether it was always distinguishable from its Irish counterpart' (Kain, p. 352).

Bibliography

Attridge, Derek, and Marjorie Howes. Eds. *Semicolonial Joyce*. Cambridge: Cambridge University Press, 2000.

Barry, Kevin. *The Dead*. Cork: Cork University Press, 2001.

Bazargan, Susan. 'The Headings in "Aeolus": a Cinematographic View.' *James Joyce Quarterly*, Vol. 23, No. 3 (Spring 1986): 345–350.

Beja, Morris. *Film & Literature: an Introduction*. New York: Longman, 1979.

Bennett, Douglas. *Encyclopaedia of Dublin*. Dublin: Gill & Macmillan, 1991.

Bennett, Thom. E-mail interview (31 March 2001). <http://www.filmthreat.com/interviews>.

Blamires, Harry. *The New Bloomsday Book: a Guide through 'Ulysses'*. Third edition. New York: Routledge, 1996.

Briggs, Austin. '"Roll Away the Reel World, the Reel World": "Circe" and Cinema'. *Coping with Joyce: Essays from the Copenhagen Symposium*, eds. Morris Beja and Shari Benstock. Columbus: Ohio State University Press, 1989. 145–156.

Burkdall, Thomas L. *Joycean Frames: Film and the Fiction of James Joyce*. New York: Routledge, 2001.

Coe, Richard L. 'Joyce Evokes a Superb Film'. *Washington Post* (15 March 1967): C11.

Cook, Louis. '"Ulysses" Is Among the Great Films, But Don't Expect a Kids' Tea Party'. *Detroit Free Press* (15 March 1967): p. 7C.

Champlin, Charles. 'Joyce's "Ulysses" Makes Film Transition'. *Los Angeles Times* (10 May 1967): 1, 16, Part IV.

Cheng, Vincent J. *Joyce, Race, and Empire*. Cambridge: Cambridge University Press, 1995.

Costello, Peter. *James Joyce: the Years of Growth 1882–1915*. New York: Pantheon, 1993.

Crist, Judith. 'A Superb Screen Translation of Joyce's "Ulysses"'. *New York Herald Tribune–Washington Post* (16 March 1967): 5.

Crowther, Bosley. Review of Joseph Strick's *Ulysses*. *New York Times* (13 March 1967): 55:1.

Cullen, Paul. 'Director Threatens Legal Action over New *Ulysses* Film'. *Irish Times* (19 June 2001), p. 25.

Devlin, Kimberly J. 'Pretending in "Penelope": Masquerade, Mimicry, and Molly Bloom'. *Molly Blooms: a Polylogue on 'Penelope' and Cultural Studies*, ed. Richard Pearce. Madison: University of Wisconsin Press, 1994: 80–102.

Duffy, Enda. *The Subaltern 'Ulysses'*. Minneapolis: University of Minnesota Press, 1994.

Dwyer, Michael. 'Strick, Bearing Bawdy Greeks, Sees "Ulysses" Come Home at Last'. *Irish Times* (November 11, 2000): W6.

Eliot, T. S. '"Ulysses," Order and Myth'. *Selected Prose of T. S. Eliot*, ed. Frank Kermode. New York: Farrar, Straus and Geroux, 1975. 175–178.

Ellmann, Richard. Ed. *Letters of James Joyce*. Vol. III. New York: The Viking Press, 1966.

——. 'Bloomovie'. *The New York Review of Books* (15 June 1967): pp. 12–13

——. *James Joyce. New and Revised Edition*. New York: Oxford University Press, 1982.

Fairhall, James. *James Joyce and the Question of History*. Cambridge: Cambridge University Press, 1993.

Gilbert, Stuart. Ed. *Letters of James Joyce*. New York: The Viking Press, 1957.

Glackin, William C. '"Ulysses" Comes Out a Superb Movie'. *The Sacramento Bee* (15 March 1967): B10.

Haigwood. '"Ulysses", Most Eloquent Cinematic Statement in Decade of Filmmaking'. *Berkely Daily Gazette* (17 March 1967): 10.

Herr, Cheryl. *Joyce's Anatomy of Culture*. Urbana: University of Illinois Press, 1986.

Hodgart, Matthew J. C., and Mabel P. Worthington. *Songs in the Work of James Joyce*. New York: Columbia University Press, 1959.

Hulme, T. E. 'Romanticism and Classicism'. *Speculations: Essays on Humanism and the Philosophy of Art*. London: Routledge and Kegan Paul, 1958. 111–140.

Joyce, James. *Dubliners*. New York: Penguin Books, 1996.

——. *Finnegans Wake*. New York: Penguin Books, 1967.

——. *A Portrait of the Artist as a Young Man*. Ed. Chester G. Anderson. New York: Viking Press, 1968.

——. *Ulysses*. Ed. Hans Walter Gabler with Wolfhard Steppe and Claus Melchior. New York: Random House, 1986.

Joyce, Stanislaus. *My Brother's Keeper*. New York: Viking Press, 1958.

Kael, Pauline. *Kiss Kiss Bang Bang*. New York: Atlantic Monthly Press Book, 1968.

Kain, Richard M. '"Ulysses" on Film'. *James Joyce Quarterly*, Vol. 4, No. 4 (Summer 1967): 351–353.

Kenner, Hugh. 'Homer's Sticks and Stones'. *James Joyce Quarterly*, Vol. 6, No. 4 (Summer 1969): 285–298.

Lawrence, Karen. *The Odyssey of Style in 'Ulysses.'* Princeton: Princeton University Press, 1981.

Loynd, Ray. '"Ulysses" – Uncompromising as a Movie'. *Los Angeles–Herald Examiner* (10 May 1967). F2.

McCormick, Kathleen. 'Reproducing Molly Bloom: a Revisionary History of the Reception of "Penelope", 1922–1970'. *Molly Blooms: a Polylogue on 'Penelope' and Cultural Studies*, ed. Richard Pearce. Madison: University of Wisconsin Press, 1994. 17–39.

Mason, Ellsworth and Richard Ellmann. Eds. *The Critical Writings of James Joyce*. Ithaca: Cornell University Press, 1989.

Murray, Edward. *The Cinematic Imagination*. New York: Frederick Ungar Publishing, 1972.

Nolan, Emer. *James Joyce and Nationalism.* London: Routledge, 1995.

Pearce, Richard. *The Novel in Motion: an Approach to Modern Fiction.* Columbus: Ohio State University Press, 1983.

Power, Arthur. *Conversations with Joyce.* Ed. Clive Hart. Chicago: University of Chicago Press, 1982.

Power, Mary. 'The Discovery of *Ruby.' James Joyce Quarterly,* Vol. 18, No. 2 (Winter 1981): 115–122.

Said, Edward W. *Orientalism.* New York: Vintage, 1978.

Segall, Jeffrey. *Joyce in America: Cultural Politics and the Trials of 'Ulysses.'* Berkeley: University of California Press, 1993.

Sicker, Philip. 'Evenings at the Volta: Cinematic Afterimages in Joyce.' Forthcoming in the *James Joyce Quarterly.*

Skeffington, Andrée D. Sheehy. 'James Joyce and "Cupid's Confidante".' *James Joyce Quarterly,* Vol. 21, No. 3 (Spring 1984): 205–214.

Spiegel, Alan. *Fiction and the Camera Eye: Visual Consciousness in Film and the Modern Novel.* Charlottesville: University Press of Virginia, 1976.

Sullivan, Robert. 'Joyce's "Ulysses" is Outstanding as Movie.' *The Capital Times* (5 March 1967): Green Section, p. 4.

Tall, Emily. 'Eisenstein on Joyce: Sergei Eisenstein's Lecture on James Joyce at the State Institute of Cinematography, November 1, 1934.' *James Joyce Quarterly,* Vol. 24, No. 2 (Winter 1987): 133–142.

Terry, Clifford. 'Controversial "Ulysses" Film Excellent.' *Chicago Tribune* (15 March 1967): Section 2, pp. 1–2.

Tindall, William York. *A Reader's Guide to 'Finnegans Wake.'* New York: Farrar, 1969.

'"Ulysses" in Parts as Great Masterpiece as Joyce Book.' *The Hollywood Reporter* (10 March 1967), p.3.

Taylor, Richard. Ed. *Beyond the Stars: the Memoirs of Sergei Eisenstein.* Trans William Powell. Calcutta: Seagull Books, 1995.

Valente, Joseph. '"Neither fish nor flesh"; or how "Cyclops" stages the double-bind of Irish manhood'. *Semicolonial Joyce,* eds. Derek Attridge and Marjorie Howes. Cambridge: Cambridge University Press, 2000: 96–127.

Van Caspel, Paul. *Bloomers on the Liffey: Eisegetical Readings of Joyce's 'Ulysses'.* Baltimore: John Hopkins University Press, 1986.

Watts, Stephen. 'Movies: "If You Censor 'Ulysses' There Will be a Scandal"'. *New York Times* (Sunday, October 2, 1966): D11.

Werner, Gösta. 'James Joyce and Sergej Eisenstein'. Trans. Erik Gunnemark. *James Joyce Quarterly,* Vol. 27, No. 3 (Spring, 1990): 491–507.

Werner, Gösta. *Nordic Rejoycings 1982: in Commemoration of the Centenary of the Birth of James Joyce.* Norberg: Uno Johansons Tryckeri AB, 1982: 125–136.

Winsten, Archer. '"Ulysses" Opens at 12 Theaters'. *New York Post* (14 March 1967): 70.

Wolf, William. '"Ulysses"'. *Cue Magazine* (25 March 1967): 49.